D1611273

THE

TYLER ROSE

The Earl Campbell Story

An Authorized Biography

As told to Paddy Joe Miller

SCHUROMIL PRODUCTIONS

SPRING, TEXAS

THE TYLER ROSE:
THE EARL CAMPBELL STORY
AS TOLD TO PADDY JOE MILLER

Copyright © 1997 by Schuromil Productions, Inc.

All rights reserved. No part of this book may be used or reproduced in any manner whatsoever without written permission, except for brief quotations embodied in critical articles or reviews.
For information contact Schuromil Productions at
17622 Surreywest Lane, Spring, Texas, 77379

Production Coordinators: Marilyn Overcast and Ronnie Bird
Final Editing, Layout and Book Design: Ron Kaye and Connie Schmidt /
Schmidt Kaye & Co.

Second Printing, October 1997

ISBN: 0-9659563-0-X

Schuromil Productions, Inc.
Printed by BookCrafters, Inc.

SPECIAL ACKNOWLEDGMENT

I want to thank my good friend Ronnie Bird for his tireless efforts in making this book possible. Because of his efforts, my life story is finally being told.

TABLE OF CONTENTS

FOREWORD

In the years since I walked off a football field for the last time, I've felt extremely fortunate. I set out, years ago, with definitive goals, and have accomplished each one. I set goals for myself not only as an athlete, but also as a man.

One of my earliest wishes was to be able to take care of my mother and family back in Tyler, and thankfully, I've been blessed with the resources to do just that. Over the years, I've been able to make numerous financial moves that have guaranteed that my family — especially my wife, Reuna, and my children, Christian and Tyler — would never be in need of anything.

Unfortunately, the success of these business endeavors came at a high price, because I seemed occupied every moment of every day. I still had challenges to meet, one of which almost drove me to an early death. I never gave serious thought to having my biography written. After all, I am still a relatively young man, with plenty of energy to meet the many obstacles before me.

Although I still maintain an extremely busy schedule, I now feel that the time is right to publish my biography. I know my story is unlike that of any other athlete's, yet it possesses elements that many people will be able to relate to. Many will remember my football statistics, both in college and professional football, but few people know the complete story. Many like me have started life out dirt poor and have fought their way to success. But not many have experienced losing their father at an early age, and then watching their mother try to raise eleven young children. Somehow she managed to do it; she overcame all the adversity that her life had dealt her, and still succeeded in teaching each of us morals and ethics, and giving us dignity as well as integrity. She has instilled in her family a firm belief in a God who truly watches over His believers.

After you read this book, I hope you realize that it's about more than football, even though I also hope you have as much fun remembering and reliving certain games and plays as I have. No doubt, there are incidents in this book that even those who know me well aren't aware of. At times, it was very difficult to relive many of the events in my past and tell them to Paddy Joe Miller, because of the pain I was forced to recall. Thanks to his patience and understanding, Paddy has done an admirable job relating those events to you.

When I say the time is right to do this biography, I truly believe this, because I want to send a message to everyone, especially young people, that life is not the proverbial bowl of cherries. Instead, it's a series of challenges that must be met, and goals that must be accomplished, in order to succeed.

Today too many of our supposed role-model athletes have lost their sense of priorities, due to the large salaries they are now able to command. In too many ways, professional football today has become a negative force in society, and I am truly concerned about this. These star athletes are featured in the media because of their huge salaries and extravagant lifestyles, not because of their unique athletic talents or contributions to society.

This biography has been ten years in the making, and first and foremost, it should be read as a tribute to my mother, Ann, and my wife, Reuna, without whom none of this could have been experienced — much less written about. Just as our country is gifted every four or eight years with different first ladies who do not rule, but gently guide, God has gifted me with two of the finest first ladies. They have helped me with all of my challenges and goals, even those that seemed virtually impossible to overcome or achieve. Because of their dedication, patience, and guidance, I firmly believe, "Whatever the human mind can conceive and believe, then it *can* achieve."

Peace and Love,
Earl Christian Campbell

INTRODUCTION
BY THE AUTHOR

The first time Earl Campbell and I met to discuss the possibility of putting his life story into words, both of us had equal amounts of apprehension. Always quiet and reserved, Earl asked few questions but weighed the answers carefully. Earl is a very private person, and by agreeing to the possibility of a biography, he was well aware that I could become one of only a few individuals who would be privy to the full story of his life. He needed assurance that I would write about Earl Christian Campbell, the man, and not just Earl Campbell, the football player. He knew there was a human-interest story to be told, and he wanted to make sure that all aspects of his life would be covered, and that his story would not just be a scrapbook of sports clippings.

At the time, I wasn't aware of Earl's hidden past, and I wondered why, after ten years away from the spotlight of the National Football League, he decided to authorize a biography that would delve infinitely deeper than the highlight films from his glory days. I also wondered, what would be the hook of this story? What would it be about this book that would capture the general public's interest?

Earl's answer to this question gave me an unprecedented respect for Earl Campbell, the man. He was the sixth of eleven children born and raised in desperate poverty. Being black and poor in the fifties' and sixties' South was not easy. He also experienced a most difficult personal obstacle when a key element of his childhood was unexpectedly swept away forever. As a result of his many tribulations, Earl became an angry young man — but he learned to take out his frustrations via the one true talent he knew of that God had given him: football. Each time he touched a football, Earl was able to forget, if only for the moment.

This is where I believed Earl Campbell's story would end; I thought that the final chapter of his biography would be his induction into the NFL Hall of Fame. In fact, however, this incident was only the beginning of what has become an ongoing story about a challenge that constantly confronts the man, and will follow him throughout the remainder of his life.

In retrospect, Earl Campbell's life paralleled mine in many ways. In each of our respective childhoods, a void was created by an absence that could never be replaced. The similarities in our life stories allowed me to get inside Earl's heart and mind and view life from his perspective. Believe me when I say that many of his experiences were most difficult to translate into words, especially those that occurred before desegregation. As a Caucasian who wasn't raised in the South — and wasn't taught to tolerate prejudice — it was difficult, at first, for me to feel and understand what American blacks went through on their quest for equality and respect. Because of my personal relationship with Earl Campbell, and my getting to know him and his story, I am a changed person.

Not only do I have a newfound respect for The Tyler Rose, whom I always had admired for his football prowess; I also now view life and people differently. It took me six months in the writing of this book to understand what forty-one years of living had not taught me. What I have learned from Earl's life story has given me an even firmer belief in a caring God who controls the destiny of mankind. I have also gained more respect for all people, regardless of circumstance or color.

After you read Earl's story, I have no doubt that you will be as moved, and as inspired, as I was by this man known as *The Tyler Rose*.

Paddy Joe Miller, May, 1997

SECTION I

THE EARLY YEARS

The Tyler Rose: The Earl Campbell Story

Earl Christian Campbell is a role model — by choice. From an early age, however, he realized, as did many athletes from his era, that becoming a role model was not a given; this honor had to be earned. Earl Campbell gained his flawless reputation on the football field by earning the respect of his teammates, his opponents, and his fans. Earl always played football the way he lived his life: with intensity and commitment. Unlike many of today's athletes, who sign multimillion dollar contracts and gain instant celebrity, Earl had to work for respect. As he looks back on his life, he realizes that becoming a role model was truly an achievement, especially considering all the stumbling blocks he encountered along the way.

The Earl Campbell story begins on the streets and in the fields of Tyler, Texas.

— PJM

Born the sixth of eleven children to B.C. (Bert) and Ann Campbell on March 29, 1955, young Earl had only four certainties staring at him as he attempted to conquer the challenges that growing up in East Texas presented.

The first of these certainties was poverty. In Tyler, Texas, there were only two classes of people in 1955: rich and poor. There was no middle class. The wealth of the upper class flowed from the earth in barrels of crude oil that was its source. This is the area of the state where "Spindletop" brought fame and fortune to Humble Oil in the early 1900's.

Most of the poor families in Jones Valley and Swann, Texas were forced to a life of meager survival, eked out working in the acres of rose fields that Tyler has been blessed with. It was here that Earl Campbell's family lived and worked. It was in this atmosphere that Earl first found his values.

Working desperately to provide for his growing family, B.C. Campbell was forced to toil in the "white man's field" Monday through Friday. He would take young sons Willie, Herbert, and Alfred with him when they were old enough to help cultivate the roses. Earl was first brought to these fields with his father and older brothers when he was five years old. Initially, he only watched and learned, but he was quickly indoctrinated into his family's workforce.

The men worked the fields until dark and then returned to their home, which was easily termed a shack by today's standards. The Campbell house had a living room, dining room, a small kitchen, and three bedrooms — for thirteen people. Eventually, a bathroom with running water was added. Until then, the Campbells, like other families in their neighborhood, used outdoor facilities. This was common for the poor people of rural East Texas, even in the mid-20th century.

After washing and eating, B.C. would leave for his night job at the local K-Mart. He did whatever was required of him to keep food on the table and clothes on his family's backs. It is easy to understand why Earl, as a very young boy, made this hard-working, devoted man his first role model. From B.C., he learned about commitment, and he learned what the term "work ethic" truly means. Earl would carry his father's lessons with him throughout his life, especially on the football field.

The second certainty Earl had to face was a deep-rooted and omnipresent prejudice. He was born and raised before desegregation took effect in the part of the country he called home. The move towards racial equality was still in its infancy, and in many parts of the South, black people still had to accept the back door of restaurants as their only entrance. Their drinking fountains and bathrooms were segregated and branded *Colored Only*. Until Rosa Parks took her stand for equality in 1955, "back of the bus" was infinitely more than a cliché.

Schools were likewise "separate but equal," which meant that the Campbells could not choose which elementary school their children would attend. All black children in the community went to Griffin Elementary. None of the children attended kindergarten; Ann Campbell didn't believe in it. After all, the male members of the family were required to be in the fields as much as possible, and the girls were needed around the house to help their mother.

Earl would be forced to accept this widespread, officially endorsed prejudice until 1970, when desegregation would finally be instituted as national policy. A change in policy, however, didn't mean that the long-held prejudices of the people would end.

Roses — hundreds of thousands of beautiful Tyler roses — were yet another certainty in the young man's life. Over time, Earl grew intimately familiar with the cultivation process, learning that a simple bush, if handled properly, could yield as many as six of these trophies of nature. Earl really had no choice but to learn about roses; the rose business was the staple by which the family was fed and clothed. It was imperative that each and every member be involved in the process.

One fond memory Earl has of these days actually centers around the occasions when his mother gave him permission to take time *off* from working the fields. On a regular basis, Allen Roberts, a good friend of the family, would drive to the Campbell house and ask Ann if "it'd be all right if Earl drove him to Louisiana," not too many miles to the east of Tyler. Mr. Roberts had taken a distinct liking to Earl and trusted him to drive safely, even though Earl wasn't of legal driving age.

Roberts, like Earl's father, had worked hard all his life, but unlike B.C., he had a couple of vices. One of these was betting at the horse track in Louisiana. He also had a fondness for drinking whiskey during those trips, relaxing while young Earl sat behind the wheel with a pillow beneath his backside to ensure that he'd be able to see over the dashboard.

Roberts would speak to Earl on these rides, pontificating about life and the many difficulties that would confront the young man. In Earl he saw a future leader of black people, and he warned him about the many evils that he must stay away from in order to blossom as

4

that leader.

One of these evils was alcohol. Warned Roberts, "Son, if you ever start drinking, always drink beer. Don't be like me and drink whiskey, because whiskey rots the brain. Pay heed to what I'm telling you because you need to understand this. You are going to do much for your people and for all of mankind!" From that moment forward, Earl heeded Mr. Roberts' counsel and never drank whiskey, only an occasional beer. He took to heart his destiny of becoming a leader and role model.

Beyond that, Roberts talked to Earl about survival in life, and what it would take for the young man to rise above his circumstances. Roberts wanted Earl to break away from poverty and prejudice and the rose fields. He continually reiterated to Earl on their trips to Louisiana that "you must take control of your own destiny," and that "only *you* can make the difference about which path your life will take."

As he drank his whiskey and looked into the young man's future, Mr. Roberts gave Earl many valuable insights about life. Earl has never forgotten these rides and the wealth of lessons he learned from Mr. Roberts. He realized even then that his friend was guiding him and alerting him to the "school of hard knocks," drawing on wisdom and experience gained over many years.

Earl learned his own firsthand lessons from that "school" early on. The journeys with Mr. Roberts were welcome breaks from the everyday reality of laboring in the treacherous heat of the rose fields. This work was extremely hard, especially for a young boy.

Poverty, prejudice, and the endless drudgery of the rose fields might have taken a substantial toll on Earl if not for the fourth and greatest certainty in his life: the unconditional love from, and for, his family. As poor as the Campbells were, love of family was the glue that held them all together. It was a love made even stronger because it was fueled by a solid belief in God, a belief by which all of the

Campbell children were raised to live and abide.

As was true of many black families in the area, the Campbells practiced the Baptist faith. On Sunday, their only day off from working the fields, the children were always taken to church services. Half the family went with B.C., and the other half went to a different service with Ann. To this day, in spite of — or perhaps because of — serious challenges to his faith, Earl firmly believes in God.

All was going according to the script that a poor black family was supposed to follow at that time: *work the white man's fields Monday through Friday, work your own on Saturday, and attend church services on Sunday.* This was never questioned by any of the children, and it became an accepted way of life for Earl and his brothers and sisters. Apart from the occasional trips with Mr. Roberts, school became Earl's only reprieve from the backbreaking work in the rose fields.

Life was hard, but there was still comfort to be found in the routines of work and faith and family. And then suddenly the family's life changed forever.

Ann Campbell recalls the next series of events with perfect clarity, as if they happened only yesterday instead of more than three decades ago. April 30, 1966 started like any other day for Ann and B.C., as the couple prepared their family for work and school. Later that evening, when B. C. returned from the fields, he told Ann that he didn't feel well; he felt drained of all energy. At first everyone believed it was a case of the flu.

Ann called for the doctor to come to their house; doctors still made house calls in those days, at least in this area. The physician she called upon was one Dr. Earl Christian Kinsey, who years before had delivered a certain baby boy and had predicted that this child would be so great that the baby should be given his name. The baby's family, of course, had obliged.

After examining B.C., Dr. Kinsey could offer no diagnosis other than that he was "simply worn out and needed rest." Up till then, "rest" just hadn't been on B.C.'s priority list. By this time in his life, all eleven children had been born, so there were thirteen mouths to feed. If B.C. had worked too long and too hard for those he loved, ignoring his own needs and dreams in the process, it was because so many precious people depended on his strength and guidance.

This time B.C. had little choice but to rest and take the medicine Dr. Kinsey prescribed. After three days, however, he wasn't making a satisfactory recovery. If anything, he was getting worse. Finally a friend of the family suggested Ann take B.C. to the emergency room. Ann was afraid to do this because money was scarce, and she didn't want to burden the family with the outrageous charges of an emergency room. Besides, B.C. flatly refused to go. But after the fifth day of declining health and another opinion by a different physician, Ann and B.C. finally yielded, and it was decided that B.C. should be taken to the hospital for tests.

On May 6, 1966, B.C. Campbell was admitted to the Tyler Medical Center, where tests showed that he had an enlarged heart and a severe kidney infection. Despite the seemingly grim results, the doctors agreed that, with proper treatment, B.C. would recover. Then on May 7th, after being helped by Ann to the restroom, B.C. had trouble getting back into bed, even with her assistance. He collapsed, felled by a massive coronary. And Ann Campbell, the mother of eleven children, was suddenly a widow, faced with the task of explaining why the God the family loved had taken away their father.

When his mother told him that his father was dead, Earl ran out to the front yard to be by himself. He was in total disbelief, and he was angry. He looked heavenward, defiantly asking the God he had been taught to love and revere, "Why? Why have you taken my father from me, when I need him so much? Why are you leaving my momma alone, with eleven children to raise?" These and many other questions went through his mind as he stared at the sky, tears of anger and loneliness streaming down his face.

At the tender age of eleven, Earl was faced with a huge void in his life, a void he would never be able to fill. He would carry this feeling of betrayal throughout his life, and though time would eventually heal most of the pain of loss, the emptiness would remain unfilled.

Earl's punishing style of football became his way of trying to fill the void. It was also a way of acting out his residual pain and anger, which had been compounded by witnessing the pain and struggle his mother had gone through. Each time Earl hit someone on defense, or was handed the ball on offense, he took it personally, in the best way he knew how, by punishing his opponent in the memory of his father. It's no exaggeration to say that Earl's win-at-all-costs attitude was the result of his anger at being cheated by his father's death.

B.C. Campbell's death propels Earl, even today, to excel in whatever he tries. Although Earl would find more role models — in fact there were to be several in his life — his father was the first and most influential. He still seeks to honor B.C.'s memory by his efforts, his work ethic, and his triumphs.

Ann Campbell now found herself shouldered with the burden of feeding a total of seventeen mouths. Shortly after B.C. died, her mother's house had burned to the ground, leaving her mother, her sister, and her sister's three children homeless. They had to join the Campbell family in that small three-bedroom house.

Along with Ann, Earl's brother Willie had inherited much of the huge family responsibility, as he was the oldest child. The youngest child was only three. But even with Willie's help, life was harder than ever.

The Early Years

Despite their grievous losses, however, one thing none of the Campbell family ever lost was their belief in God. Even after being tested so severely, their faith remained as strong as ever. After a time, even Earl stopped asking *why*, and began trying to deal with his anger and loss. His bitterness slowly turned into acceptance that God controls the destiny of all lives and souls with a wisdom we may not always understand.

Even so, as Earl entered his fifth-grade school year he was still consumed by shock and grief over his father's death. Fortunately, a new role model was soon to enter his life. It was at Griffin Elementary School that Earl first met Thorndike Lewis, a young teacher with a true love for the students he taught. Lewis introduced sports to fifth and sixth grade boys, taking on the enormous task of being the football, basketball, and baseball coach, while at the same time driving the school bus. He accepted all of these responsibilities on his own, with never a thought given to his limited salary. "I did it for the kids," he says simply.

It was under the guidance of Thorndike Lewis that Earl Christian Campbell joined his first "true" football team and became the kicker for the Griffin Elementary Cowboys. The unique twist to this fifth and sixth grade level football was that it was "flag" football — that is, each player wore two flags, one on each hip, and a person had to be stripped of his flag in order to consider the play dead.

In his first year playing football, the future Heisman Trophy winner and NFL Hall of Famer wouldn't be stripped of many flags, as the only thing he was asked to do was kick the football. That hardly mattered, though; what mattered was that from the first play Earl became involved in, an immediate rush came over him — a rush that made him feel good. It was a very natural feeling for the young man. More than that, it was a revelation, for it was then that Earl Campbell realized God had put him on this earth to excel at football.

Thorndike Lewis became the first of many coach role models

for Earl and, as he looks back on it now, he realizes that in many ways, the coach saved his life. Coach Lewis instilled in Earl a love for the game, especially in sixth grade when Earl became "The Man." Lewis took a keen interest in his players and made sure that the sport they were playing occupied them, thereby keeping them out of trouble.

This was particularly important in Earl's case, for, although a relatively trouble-free student in the fifth and sixth grade, he was prone to complacency, especially in his studies. Without football, he could have become involved in other less desirable "extracurricular" activities, as did so many of his peers. He could easily have fallen into a lifestyle whose end result was his own destruction. In retrospect, Coach Lewis truly did save the young man's life. Although Earl wouldn't realize it until much later, Lewis had become the first of many "guardian angels" in his life. Earl still maintains a tremendous amount of respect for Thorndike Lewis.

When Earl reached sixth grade, Thorndike was impressed with his work ethic and began playing him full time at middle linebacker and running back. This was in addition to his duties as kicker. Even at that early point in Earl's life, he knew one thing for certain: he'd rather hit than be hit. He fell in love with the middle linebacker position, and fancied himself to be another Dick Butkus, who was his hero on the gridiron. He took to emulating Butkus' walk, letting anyone he played with or against know, "There ain't none badder than Dick Butkus!" Or perhaps there were none badder than Earl Campbell. In the sixth grade, Earl was already immense — almost as big as he is today, in fact. He was a very feared *hombre.*

With his impressive size as a linebacker, Earl's prowess as a running back didn't get much attention. Even so, this flag football era provided a hint of the future, for during this time Earl developed one of his first real talents: effective use of a stiff-arm. Eventually he would learn to use this stiff-arm with brutal precision, as many an NFL defensive player can readily testify. In the beginning, however, the stiff-arm was sheer expediency for Earl. Because flag football revolves around "keeping your flags on while running the football," he began to avoid oncoming defensive players with his long, straight, muscled-up forearm. Without even knowing or caring at the time, young Earl was a natural at running the ball.

Coach Lewis perceived this natural talent. He particularly admired Earl's offensive skills, which he sensed would destine the boy for football greatness. Campbell had the ability to run around — or over — the opposition, whichever seemed proper at the time. He was big. He was strong. He was fast. He could *move* the football. In all of Lewis' subsequent years of coaching, no athlete would linger more predominantly in his mind than Earl Campbell, and Lewis would encounter many future superstars.

When asked what he saw in Earl Campbell as his greatest single quality, Coach Lewis took a few minutes to reflect before responding. "The finest quality that I saw in Earl didn't have anything to do with football. Earl's finest quality was that he always put his mother first out of respect and devotion. This character trait was ingrained in him as a young boy because of his quality family upbringing.

"After B.C. Campbell passed away, Earl was forced to assume many responsibilities, aside from playing football. He took the values that were passed on to him by his father, and learned to make a stepping stone out of each stumbling block he encountered. Earl always got the job handled, *whatever* it was, hurt or not, and did it all with his momma at the forefront of his thoughts. In many ways, Earl was a visionary. He knew what he wanted in life and worked untiringly toward achieving these goals."

Coach Lewis summed up Earl Campbell at age twelve: "Watching Earl Campbell play football was almost as good as going to heaven, because of the overall qualities he displayed."

The Tyler Rose: The Earl Campbell Story

To be sure, Earl Campbell's blue jeans went through numerous iron-on patches while he was refining his skills at flag football. Inside the young man, a fire had been kindled, and it all had to do with hitting other football players *"with full pads on!"* As Earl began junior high, he also began a new phase in his early football career: hitting other people, and hitting them hard. Earl was massive in the seventh grade; he feared no one, but was feared by many. In full pads, Earl appeared even more enormous and was even more feared.

The flags were a thing of his past.

Dogan Junior High was still segregated in 1968 when Earl began the seventh grade. He looked forward to proving himself via football. He also entered that school with a different attitude than the one he'd displayed to Coach Lewis.

George McDowell, Earl's teacher and head football coach, observed, "Earl was no longer disciplined and quiet. In fact, he was downright rambunctious to those who had to teach and coach him. He became quite a prankster in the seventh grade, always happy and fun-loving. Outside of playing football, Earl wasn't very serious back then. However, once he took to that field, watch out, because Earl had to be the best!"

And he was.

Earl played that first year as an offensive and defensive lineman, loving every minute of it. He was enormous compared to those he lined up against, and he simply overpowered anyone he came in contact with. He had size, speed, and strength. Because of his age, however, he was still somewhat uncoordinated in his lateral movements. As a lineman, Earl would learn a great deal from the lateral drills that he was forced to use.

In eighth grade, Earl's personality as a prankster really bloomed. According to Coach McDowell, "Earl sure took a lot of spankings from me back in those days." This was done with the tacit permission of Ann Campbell, who made it well known to the teachers that if any of her children got out of line, they had permission to discipline that child in the best way they saw fit. Between the teachers and their momma, the Campbell children were kept in line pretty well. Of course, Momma Campbell was no one to mess with either, since she had seen it all.

Or had she?

It turns out that Ann Campbell wasn't made aware, until many years after the fact, that the prank of all pranks had been played by Earl and his twin brothers, Tim and Steve. What's more, they got away with it. Then as now, all students who wanted to get involved in athletics must obtain written permission from their parents. Earl knew that Momma Campbell wouldn't allow him to play tackle football, because of the risk of injury. She didn't want to jeopardize his future work in the rose fields, especially with B.C. gone. Given their desperate family situation, Ann needed all the children's help. Considering the number of people living under that one small roof, it was no surprise that she was concerned.

In the end, however, the twins forged Momma Campbell's signature to Earl's permission slip, and he did the same to theirs. Next they went to Dr. Kinsey, who immediately declared them healthy enough to play football. But you can't keep a secret from your momma for long, and when the boys began coming home later and later at the beginning of football practice, she knew *something* was up. Eventually, they told her the truth about playing tackle football, but not about the signatures — well, at least not until much later in their lives.

As a student in the eighth grade, Earl made only marginal grades. George McDowell, who continued to coach and discipline the young man, firmly believed Earl was too much prankster and not enough student. Then on one particular day, as the coach sat in his office overlooking the field, he witnessed a quality in Earl Campbell that he'd never seen before, one that was simply unbelievable. As many players this age so often do, Earl and his buddies were warming up by playing "tackle the man with the ball." The object is simple enough: six or more youths try to tackle one man.

When the ball was put in Earl's hands, an amazing thing happened, right in front of Coach McDowell's eyes: *no one could tackle Earl.* This happened not just once but repeatedly. Oftentimes, Earl would go through six or seven tackles before becoming bored and turning the ball over to someone else so he could then hit them.

Coach McDowell proclaimed, "I believe it's time we let Earl run the ball."

And run he did, from that point forward in his career, although he wouldn't be convinced that he truly loved running the ball until his senior year in high school. Earl's size rendered it virtually impossible for any single player to bring him down. In only one year's time in junior high, Earl completely changed positions yet again. This time he switched to positions he thoroughly enjoyed: defensive middle linebacker and offensive back. He was much more effective as a middle linebacker; Dick Butkus was still his football idol, and Earl continued to emulate the hard-hitting middle linebacker's walk.

From the time Earl began playing football for Dogan Junior High till the time he graduated from John Tyler High School, he never once stopped playing both offense and defense. This was truly an amazing feat in itself. It seemed the only time Earl *wasn't* involved in a play was during time-outs, since he also played on all special teams. Very few athletes have the stamina to sustain this level of play, but Earl did it and still managed to walk home three miles from school every day after practice with brothers Tim and Steve.

It was obvious to the casual observer, but especially to Coach McDowell, that Earl Campbell was truly born to play football. McDowell recalls Earl's greatest quality: "He wanted to excel at all levels, *always,* especially since he was bigger and stronger than everyone else. Earl tried to play basketball for me in the eighth grade; however, he played that sport the way he played football — *all out* — and usually fouled out by the third quarter. Earl's desire to compete was so intense that I *knew* he had the talent it takes to go far. The problem was getting him serious enough to understand that!"

Earl was going to need every bit of his size and strength as he entered his freshman year at his first integrated school, Moore Junior High, in 1970. This was a very tumultuous time in our country's history. Not only was a controversial war being waged on the other side of the world, but at home, racial tensions were at an all time high. The civil rights activism of the fifties had given way to the race riots of the late sixties, and in the seventies the government decided to force the issue by implementing busing in many areas of the country. America was a boiling cauldron of racial violence, and Earl Campbell found himself right in the middle of it.

Two big influences would enter Earl's life his freshman year: prejudice, and a man named Lawrence "Butch" La Croix. The latter made the former more bearable. It was La Croix, more than anyone, who helped the young adolescent deal with the reality of racial problems in his new school. And an admirable job he did, particularly considering it was his first year as a teacher and coach in this predominately white school.

This was an era that Earl freely admits was his teenage "Bad Earl stage." Things were different for him now. He realized he would have to earn his respect, instead of accepting it as a given due to his size. Although his Dogan Junior High School team had been the eighth-grade football champs the previous year, he would have to start the respect process all over again. And this time it would be more difficult, for now there were people who would hold a grudge against him because of his color. This is where Coach La Croix stepped in to help the young man, as he did all of his players, acting out of love for both the game and his students.

The Tyler Rose: The Earl Campbell Story

In Coach Lawrence La Croix, Earl found another role model. When Earl was desperately in need of discipline, and the school was entrenched in prejudice, Coach La Croix helped to defuse the hatred and anger that was prevalent in both the blacks and whites of Moore Junior High.

The white students had a student named David Wells as their tacit leader. It was simply understood that he was their spokesperson. The black students had Earl — big, bad, and, to tell the truth, a little frightened. After all, the numbers were definitely in favor of the white populace at the school.

Wells was on the football team. Like Earl, he was big in stature, and he pulled an extreme amount of weight — literally as well as figuratively — with his fellow white students. Because Earl was the expressed leader of the black students, everyone knew that a fight between him and David was going to happen sooner or later. The question was not a matter of *if* as much as *when*.

When the clash did finally break out, Wells and Campbell got into it, seemingly over nothing, and a dog-eat-dog fistfight ensued. The fight had the potential to blow the racial tension at the school sky high but, ironically, it served to ease the tensions instead. It was one of those fights where no one lost. And after the fighting and bleeding was finished, Butch La Croix brought both boys together for a heart-to-heart talk. Reconciliation was especially important, he let them know, since they were going to be playing on the same team together.

Said Coach La Croix to the boys, "With the direction our current situation is headed, the two of you will make the difference. You both must learn to represent the name of our school, not the color of the person present." It was to be Earl's mission to spread this word among the black students, and David Wells' to the white students. Coach La Croix knew the only way both sides could successfully learn to coexist was if they worked at it together.

16

The Early Years

Oddly enough, after Coach La Croix had his "Come to Jesus Meeting" with Earl Campbell and David Wells, the two became best of friends. Working together, they eventually united all the students, as well as their parents, toward one common goal: winning a state championship trophy for John Tyler High School.

Before the quest for the championship could begin, however, Earl had to complete his freshman year. Once again he played both middle linebacker and tailback, and as usual, his drive to excel was unsurpassed. Earl and Coach La Croix developed a unique connection, and in the process it became evident that Coach La Croix was yet another of Earl's guardian angels. It didn't take a great leap of faith to believe this man had been sent to watch over Earl, to discipline him, and to get inside his mind.

For Butch La Croix seemed to have the uncanny ability to read Earl and his thoughts. Perhaps more than most, he realized how much the death of B.C. had affected young Earl, and he sensed the deep impressions left on Earl by the poverty his family had endured. In short, he recognized the loneliness and hurt inside the young man. Butch La Croix stepped into Earl's life at exactly the right time, when he was vulnerable and needed a father figure, a role model, and someone who could once again fill the boy's need for a hero.

Earl's freshman year was one in which he matured greatly, in no small part from Coach La Croix's many valuable lessons about life and football. La Croix taught Earl about keeping the events of life in perspective. He believed that all things happened for a reason and were willed by God.

And yet Coach La Croix confided on several occasions to his wife, Ann, that he feared he wasn't getting through to Earl. At times, Earl simply didn't seem to be listening to him. As perceptive as La Croix was, in this one area he was wrong, for Earl *did* listen to him. He absorbed every word the coach ever told him, especially those lessons relating to the value of humility.

Earl learned about humility on the day he scored his first touchdown in the ninth grade, during an inner-team scrimmage. He was lined up as the tailback on offense and took a pitchout, untouched, the length of the field. As he scored, the future star did his best "Elmo Wright imitation," patterned after the Kansas City Chiefs' star. He "strutted his stuff" into the end zone, football firmly in hand.

After witnessing this most unusual bit of chicanery from Earl, La Croix took him aside for one of the many lessons he would teach the young warrior. La Croix pointed out to Earl, in no uncertain terms, that those who were watching him play football didn't need to be reminded, via a shabby 'hot dog' imitation, that he had scored a touchdown. "After all," the coach pointed out, "handling success with humility is every bit as important as accepting failure with grace."

Earl took that lesson to heart. After that, whenever he scored a touchdown — and there were many — he either laid the ball promptly on the ground or handed it to the referee. There was no fancy strutting, no in-your-face taunting. When Earl Campbell scored, his teammates, his opponents, and his fans were all fully aware not only of his grit as an athlete, but of his dignity as a man.

From that day forward, when Earl Campbell scored, it was done with *class*.

As a matter of fact, there was virtually nothing Earl wouldn't do to please Coach La Croix, although the coach still privately confided to his wife that he didn't know if he was "getting through to the young man." He needn't have worried. Earl's career and life are a testament to the fact that Butch La Croix was indeed getting through — both on and off the field.

On the field, Earl broke his hand early in the year, and the break required a cast. This didn't put a damper on his burning desire to excel, "no matter what the cost." Foremost in Earl's mind was the thought that he couldn't let Coach La Croix or the team down; in the end, he went to the shop classroom and cut the cast off. Earl played that entire year with a broken hand, vowing never to wear a cast on his hand again. It was a promise he was to keep throughout his entire career.

Earl's freshman year would also find him influenced in another very special way, and this influence would be with him for the rest of his life. On the first day he arrived at Moore Junior High, he spotted Reuna Smith standing underneath two enormous trees in front of the school. She was one of 175 black students who'd been sent to Moore. The attraction was instant, it was powerful, and, best of all, it was mutual. Reuna confessed, many years later, that Earl seemed to give off a "halo effect." She admits she was awestruck that first day she saw him step off the bus. For the next thirteen years, Reuna would be Earl's girlfriend, high school sweetheart, and best friend. She finally became his wife, and they continue to be inseparable.

Now young Earl had someone else to play for besides his family. Each time he stepped onto the field, he wanted to impress this beautiful young woman. As Earl sees it, Reuna had to have been another guardian angel sent to him. She set about, with the constant guidance of Coach La Croix, to instill discipline in the young man's life. Between Reuna and Coach La Croix, they did an excellent job.

Unfortunately, Coach La Croix was not available to be interviewed for this book. Butch La Croix had a massive coronary and died in 1979. Before he passed away, however, Earl would still have many good years with the young coach. Through college and some of his pro career, Earl was blessed with his influence and guidance.

Coach La Croix's widow, Ann, heard much about Earl from her husband. She also got to know him personally as he matured and grew mentally and emotionally, and she had these words to say about Earl: "Even at that early stage of his life, Earl could see the big picture, and he would let nothing get in his way. He was convinced of his destiny."

In this instance, a young man did listen, and as a result he understood that he needed to stay on the straight and narrow, refining the skills that would take him to great heights. Even at an early age, Earl Campbell knew in his soul that he was going to excel in football, and that he would do it in an amazing fashion. Coach La Croix had truly done his job and made a man out of the kid, letting a clean conscience and bone-jarring football be his guide.

Earl Campbell would be confronted with many issues, virtually overnight, as he exited from adolescence into manhood. Racial tension was still running high, but somehow Earl, with the help of David Wells, got everyone through it in that first crucial year.

As much of a challenge as Moore Junior High had been, in a way it was just a warm-up for the milieu Earl was to enter into at John Tyler High School. Gone would be the constant positive reinforcement of Coach La Croix; Earl would be faced with a new curriculum, totally new coaches and a whole new "set of rules."

Once in high school, Earl would be challenged in many areas, each more intense than the last. He would be forced to learn to wear many different hats as he strove to maintain order in a system that was having a difficult time grasping one simple concept: *all men truly are created equal in the eyes of God, and are therefore deserving of equal respect.*

Once again, Earl would have to strive to earn respect — for himself and, by extension, for black people. And once again, he would earn it by playing football.

SECTION II

HIGH SCHOOL

The Tyler Rose: The Earl Campbell Story

Earl Campbell entered high school during a time of unfolding events. It was a time when white people were forced to deal with blacks in new social, academic, religious, and economic situations.

The tensions that were brewing when Earl had entered junior high were still as strong as ever. Earl recalled Lawrence La Croix's words to him: "You will make a difference — both on the field and off." These words were showing themselves to be prophetic again as Earl once more assumed the leadership role. This time an entire school looked to him for his strength and guidance in defusing a potentially ugly situation. Amazingly enough, it would be football that brought the city of Tyler, Texas together. This unity was inspired by a high school football team's goal: a state championship trophy for John Tyler High School.

— PJM

From the very start of his sophomore year, Earl was a troubled young man. He knew that in the current atmosphere, there would be much added pressure on all of the black students to prove themselves worthy of the "equality" which many of the whites felt was being jammed down their throats. Ever sensitive to Earl's moods, Reuna became aware early that summer that something very deep was bothering Earl, causing his attitude to lean even more towards complacency. It was something no one could place a finger on, yet it was almost palpable.

As a matter of fact, it was a feeling Earl had experienced only a few years before, at the time when his father passed away. The truth was that Earl was once again feeling a sense of loss, and this time it was due to the absence of his coach and surrogate father, Lawrence La Croix, who was, of course, still at Earl's old junior high. Earl later stated that the coach was "someone I'd have wanted my father to be like, if he were alive." Perhaps because Earl had trouble expressing himself in those days, the older man didn't realize the depth of Earl's admiration for him, or the extent of the boy's need for guidance and stability beyond La Croix's coaching expertise.

That they had become friends, though, was undeniable. In the summer between ninth and tenth grade, Reuna and Earl had visited the coach and his wife regularly. On those long, lazy evenings after the day's work in the rose fields, Earl would eagerly come with his girl to the La Croix home, seeking companionship as well as guidance. The four of them would sit on the front porch, drinking tea, laughing and gossiping. That summer, Earl's dreams had seemed as elusive to him as the dim shadows crawling across the dirt road leading to town.

Now school had started, and a familiar and enormous void was in Earl's heart once again. Things just weren't the same without Coach La Croix. As a result, Earl elected to be a no-show for fall practice. Football season was approaching, but Earl seemed to have lost his edge. Even his anger — that passion which had fueled his need to punish others on the field — seemed to be gone.

When, at the urging of La Croix, Earl finally decided to report to football practice, he most assuredly didn't get the reception he had anticipated. First year head coach Corky Nelson, unaware of the young man's talents, was so deeply unimpressed with Earl's feeble attempt at explaining why he hadn't reported with the rest of the team, that he almost sent him home for the entire season. Fortunately, however, he told Earl that he would allow him to practice — but it would have to be on the B team, under the auspices of George Craddock.

Craddock was a tough, no-nonsense coach who *was* aware of Earl's prowess and knew what the boy could do with a football. He utilized the young athlete to his greatest potential, at both middle linebacker and running back. During this time, however, he wasn't cognizant of the change that had come over Earl, never having witnessed the "edge" that had always been so prevalent in Earl's demeanor. Earl had become a quiet, reserved student and player, and, ironically, this was happening at a time when he was also emerging as a leader.

Naturally, many felt that what the students *didn't* need was a "quiet, reserved Earl." But none of these people realized that what they were getting in exchange was a more mature person, someone who had grown mentally and emotionally. And this was due largely to the independence fostered by Coach La Croix.

Most of the time Earl still kept his feelings inside, letting his football do the talking. Even Reuna, his best friend, couldn't understand the hurt inside him as he went through the motions, striving to be an asset to an inferior team. He just didn't communicate much. In many ways, Earl was a mystery even to those closest to him.

Coach Craddock was enjoying a 5-0 early season record, due, in large part, to the play of Earl Campbell. On the other hand, Corky Nelson was 0-5 in his first season, and feeling pressure from the hometown crowd. As luck would have it — for both Corky and Earl — the starting varsity middle linebacker went down with a season-ending injury. Because of this, Earl was taken from Coach Craddock and his team's perfect record, and reassigned to the starting middle linebacker position on the varsity team.

Little could Coach Nelson have known at the time that this move would propel him and his team to a much better season record, planting them firmly upon the path to the school's future greatness.

The remainder of Nelson's initial coaching season wasn't at all memorable, except for the closing record. After a 0-5 start, followed by Earl's insertion into the starting lineup, the team went 4-0-1. In his very first varsity game against Longview, Earl was credited with six quarterback sacks. He was also honored as Newcomer of the Year, with only five games played.

That's how much of an impact Earl had on the teams he played with and against.

And now it seemed that Earl was changing once again. After his sophomore year, Coach Nelson noticed a degree of "cockiness" about him. There was no doubt in the coach's mind that Earl had developed something of an attitude. As for the type of attitude, and, more importantly, the reason behind it — well, neither Nelson nor anyone else was exactly sure. It is only now, after looking back on those early years, that Earl realizes his demeanor reflected an absence of guidance — the guidance that only a strong father figure can give.

Earl and Reuna were still spending many weekends at the home of Ann and Butch La Croix, especially since Reuna now had her license and could drive there whenever they had some free time. Earl was glad he could see his old coach more often now, but he still wasn't quite satisfied. "If only," he thought to himself many times, "Coach La Croix would be brought over to John Tyler. *Then,* I could become an all-around, complete ballplayer!"

Once again, as luck, or perhaps God, would have it, Earl's wishes were about to come true.

There are several schools of thought concerning the reason that Lawrence La Croix was offered a job at John Tyler High School. Coach Craddock, hard-nosed as he is, insists it was because the school needed another black teacher/coach to fill a quota. Coach Nelson states that he can't remember the circumstances that led to La Croix being brought from the junior to the senior high. Earl Campbell and Ann La Croix, however, see it differently. There is no doubt in either of their minds that La Croix was hired at John Tyler High School not to fill a quota, but rather, to fill a "patriarchal" role for Earl as part of some Divine plan. Whatever the reason — plan or accident, divine or mundane — Earl's heart leapt when he heard the news. Once again he would have his surrogate father to play for, someone who could truly be proud of his "son's" accomplishments.

Corky Nelson had Earl primed to play tailback in addition to middle linebacker during his junior year. Unfortunately, no one would get to see Earl's offensive skills until the sixth game, because Earl had suffered a severely sprained ankle during a pre-season scrimmage. Earl just couldn't depend on the flexibility of his ankle for his offensive game. He was limited at middle linebacker, although he did play this key defensive position in all ten games. Restricted by his ankle injury, he would only play the last five games of the season on offense, excelling in each one. But it wasn't enough, as two early season losses placed the team at 8-2 and out of the playoff picture. This was a time in high school football when only the district champion went to the playoffs.

Earl was named All American middle linebacker that year, but it didn't mean much to him without the team's achieving their ultimate goal of winning the state championship trophy. In what would become standard practice throughout his career, he downplayed his award, choosing instead to elevate the play of his teammates. This was not false modesty, but, more than likely, Earl's preference to focus on the team rather than on himself.

Perhaps the best thing that happened to Earl that year was a situation where he learned a valuable lesson from Corky Nelson. Over time, Coach Nelson had assumed the bad-guy role in Earl's life, while Coach La Croix, understandably, became the good guy. Earl's lesson happened on the day of the Tyler Lee game, which has always been considered by those who follow Tyler sports to be the "Super Bowl" of East Texas high school football. To this day, there is no love lost in the bitter rivalry between these two schools.

At the time Earl was playing, racial tensions often led to fights between students at the opposing schools. About the only place anything was settled between the schools was on the gridiron, in a game played once a year, with the winner earning town bragging rights that were good till the next year's battle.

On this particular Friday, as on the past nine Fridays, a pep rally was held during the first, second, and third period classes. The game against Lee was always the last of the year and, as such, added to the intensity around the school and community. For some reason, Earl, along with four other starters on the team, chose to skip fourth period, opting to goof off instead. Unknown to them, their teachers did notice they were gone, and reported their absence to the principal, Alvin Anderson. Anderson in turn made Corky Nelson aware of the problem.

This put Nelson in a difficult dilemma. If he disciplined these players the way he deemed proper and as the rules dictated, it could be viewed with racial overtones, since all the players happened to be black. Yet if he chose to ignore it, Coach Nelson would have compromised his own staunch principles, and would probably *still* be accused of making a racially-biased decision — this time, by the white players.

Nelson cursed his five players in perhaps the biggest "dressing-down" of his illustrious coaching career, and suspended all of them from playing in the game — including his All American middle linebacker. He cited district policy, which stated: "If a player fails to appear at his classes, he is then ineligible to play."

At first, Earl was incensed and threatened to quit football his senior year in order to protest the injustice dealt him. But Alvin Anderson told Earl that if he quit, he could not attend John Tyler, since playing football and going to school went hand in hand. In other words, if Earl didn't wish to play football his senior year, he could find somewhere else to finish his education.

After many discussions with Coach La Croix, Earl decided to stay and play, but not before Ann Campbell told Coach Nelson how she felt about the situation.

"Coach," she began, "I don't mind you disciplining my Earl. You have my total support on that. However, you have no right to cuss at him or the other boys the way you did, and I won't tolerate that any longer — from you, or anyone else!"

After much thought, Nelson realized that Ann was right, and he apologized to the five players. Not only did this wise woman steer Earl in the right direction about life and about keeping football in perspective, she also enlightened Coach Nelson. As it so happened, that was the first time in his career that Nelson had cursed at any of his players, and after Ann Campbell talked with him, it was the last. Thanks to her wisdom, Coach Nelson never again had to apologize to his players for any of his actions.

For his part, Earl learned a valuable lesson in humility from Coach Nelson, as he was unable to play in the all-important Lee game. Nevertheless John Tyler defeated Lee 6-0 in a driving rain, with the only touchdown being scored by Lynn King. The lasting result of the incident was that Earl, truly embarrassed by his foolish behavior and the consequent punishment, never forgot this lesson. He was well-served by its memory as he made his way through life.

By the beginning of Earl's senior year, it was apparent to those who knew him that he had matured in all aspects. Gone were the cockiness and the weird attitude. Earl had grown much surer of himself, and knew where he wanted to go with his life.

Earl and a white player named Lynn King were successfully bringing together the people of Tyler on the final step toward the quest for a state football championship. All the necessary elements were coming together: the city, the coaches, and a definitive combination of players. Although the team was young, with many sophomores and juniors, they were led by the formidable maturity and discipline of Campbell and King.

This would be the first year that Earl wasn't called upon to play middle linebacker full-time, having earned the spotlight as a running back. At first, he didn't understand or appreciate being placed in the running back position full-time. He still maintained his Butkus-like attitude and swagger. Besides that, he wanted a chance to play alongside his twin brothers, Tim and Steve, who were starting at the outside linebacker positions. Earl really didn't like the fact that he would only be used on defense in special situations, and proved this by intentionally fumbling the ball at the line of scrimmage during practice.

In the end, however, Coaches Nelson and La Croix convinced him to concentrate upon his running career, in lieu of focusing upon his defensive prowess. This was sage advice. Unknown to virtually everyone involved in Earl's career, Corky Nelson had already been talking to Ken Dabbs, the East Texas recruiter for The University of Texas at Austin. After listening to Nelson and viewing Earl on the practice field, Dabbs privately confided to Nelson that Earl was too small to be middle linebacker at a major college level. However, based on what he saw of Earl's running abilities, he felt that Earl stood a much better chance of being recruited for The University of Texas as a running back. After hearing Dabbs' opinion about Earl, Nelson was convinced that his decision was a good one, especially since he planned on giving Earl the ball an average of 35 times a game.

Having overcome many difficult challenges, and with so many hard-earned lessons under his belt, Earl was now mentally capable of leading both the football team and his schoolmates. And lead them he did. Racial tensions notwithstanding, he managed to keep the students focused upon the goal of a state championship.

Throughout this time, Reuna was a constant companion and friend, always making sure Earl kept out of trouble. With her care and concern, and the guidance of Coach La Croix and his wife, Earl maintained passing grades in his schoolwork — an absolute necessity if he planned to pursue college football.

Although this was an intensely demanding time in Earl's life, he was, with the help of his various and valued guardian angels, more than ready for the obstacles that would confront him as he forged his path upon a career that would ultimately lead to greatness.

In Earl's senior year, the John Tyler Lions opened against Greenville with a very young, inexperienced offensive line. About the only consistency the team had was the combination of Earl at tailback,

The Tyler Rose: The Earl Campbell Story

Lynn King at fullback, and Larry Hartsfield, a third year starter, at quarterback. Their offensive backfield was the strength of Corky Nelson's attack. The defense, led by junior linebackers Steve and Tim Campbell, was also young but definitely capable of holding their own on the field.

Although John Tyler won the Greenville game 20-0, Earl endured a very tough and physical game, taking many punishing hits. But after each hit, Earl continued to encourage the young linemen, reassuring them that they were doing fine and that they'd all get better as time went on. Even though he was getting pummeled play after play, Earl kept this encouragement up for the duration of the game.

This is what Coach Nelson ultimately remembers as the greatest quality in Earl. "He had a certain humility about himself," Nelson explains. "He constantly built up the people around him with encouragement and support, always at his own expense. He *never* chastised anyone."

With this humble strength, Earl became the team leader, winning respect even from Lynn King, as Tyler continued its quest for statewide renown. By his final year of high school, Earl Campbell had become "The Man."

John Tyler finished the regular season undefeated. The season ended with a resounding defeat of Tyler Lee, which meant, of course, that the year's city bragging rights went to John Tyler.

Opponents would often remark about Earl's unusually low center of gravity, which, coupled with intense speed, made it extremely difficult to bring him down. These assets, combined with great flexibility in his ankles, knees, and hips, made Earl a virtual nightmare to confront in a one-on-one situation. About the only part of Earl's body that could be hit effectively was his shoulder pads, and this was a source of great frustration to the defensive players he faced.

High School

With the Lee defeat, John Tyler had succeeded in clearing their first hurdle on the road to the state championship, but there was still much ground to cover with five playoff games ahead. Beginning in the third week of November 1973, the entire city of Tyler banded together as one in what would become the school's greatest single achievement, scholastics notwithstanding. All people — black and white, young and old, even those from rival schools — got on this very formidable bandwagon. After three years of extreme tension — racial and otherwise — the hard work of Coaches Nelson and La Croix, Earl Campbell, Lynn King, and all the rest of the players, was coming to fruition. In the city of Tyler, Texas, football became the element of relief that could overshadow prejudices and misunderstandings among the citizens.

In their first playoff game, John Tyler played at home in Rose Stadium, thanks to Coach Nelson having won the coin toss. That was how these matters were decided. Their opponent would be Plano, a powerhouse from outside Dallas to whom they had already lost in a pre-season scrimmage. Because that game was a scrimmage, however, it meant nothing in the statistics. Earl was well aware of this as he prepared for "show time." In this playoff game, he was dead-solid serious about winning, and gained over 250 yards rushing, literally crushing the opposing team, 24-7. The game was a true "whooping," as Earl reflects back, and it was also the game in which he became aware that God truly had given him a purpose and a talent. As a result of this epiphany, he committed himself to utilizing this talent to the best of his ability for the remainder of his life.

In the next game, John Tyler faced an unbeaten team from Conroe. Of this team, Coach Nelson observed, "They were big, fast, and blew through their division with a vengeance." The game was to be played in Conroe, just to the north of Houston, because this time, Nelson lost the coin toss.

The game was extraordinarily physical and bruising, and Earl was knocked unconscious early in the second half. Although he managed to finish the game with over 200 yards rushing, he missed most of the third and fourth quarters. Unbelievably, he inserted himself into the game for Tyler's last offensive possession, when his team was behind 10-7. Of the nine plays on that last offensive drive, Earl Campbell carried the ball eight times and scored the winning touchdown — even though he had a mild concussion.

That game-defining drive gave Corky Nelson a deeper understanding of Earl Campbell and his burning desire to win against all odds. His play in this game led Coach Nelson to declare that Earl was "the most outstanding athlete I've ever coached." This was the ultimate compliment for a high school athlete to receive, especially considering the plethora of great players whom Nelson had the privilege to coach over the course of his career.

Coach Nelson once again lost the coin toss for John Tyler's game against Arlington Heights, and they played in Dallas. Arlington Heights had the future professional star, Mike Renfro, who would eventually become Earl's teammate on the Houston Oilers, as their "top gun." They decided to key their entire defense against Earl, and, as a result, Lynn King benefited from their averted attention and had a huge game. Holding Earl to under 200 yards was a real feat for Arlington, considering he had finished with over a thousand yards rushing in the five playoff games that year. John Tyler was once again successful with a 34-12 victory, though the game was much closer than the final score reflected.

The next game against Arlington Sam Houston was Tyler's semi final game, held at a neutral site at Baylor stadium in Waco. Once again, Earl powered out over 200 yards rushing. His punishing style left Arlington's defensive team hurting for many days to come. This is where his extremely effective stiff-arm, learned from those early days playing flag football, came into its own. Combined with his low-to-the-ground running style of play, it was just too much for the opposing team. Earl Campbell amazed those watching him with his balance and speed, as well as the fact that it usually took more than one player to bring him down. Those who were cheering for Arlington Sam Houston were no less amazed than the Tyler fans. John Tyler won the game 21-7, and the team found themselves well on the way to their first state championship — with Earl Campbell leading them into battle.

There was more than a bit of irony in the fact that Earl would play the state championship final against Austin Reagan at the Astrodome in Houston. Of course, he had no way of knowing then that he was playing against a team whose city he would soon call home, in a stadium that he would eventually rule for six glorious years.

It was in this game that Ken Dabbs, after many months of scouting Earl Campbell, would finally have a chance to show his prospect to Darrell Royal. Royal, the well-known guru of college football and head coach of the famed University of Texas Longhorns, would finally get to see Earl play. It was to be an unforgettable night for many people, not the least of which was Earl Campbell as he rushed for over 200 yards — once again — in a hard-fought, 21-14 victory.

John Tyler had worked their way to the Texas State Championship undefeated, and stayed there, because of the awesome running ability of a young athlete who had yet to really hit his stride.

As Coaches Dabbs and Royal entered the John Tyler locker room, Darrell Royal's gaze fell upon a young man standing alone, victorious, and proud in his moment of glory. Royal saw, in the Tyler locker room that night, the perfect physical stature of a great running back: Earl Christian Campbell. Despite the fact that he was physically mature, the young man Darrell Royal met was a very quiet and shy person. Royal could tell Earl lacked confidence in himself everywhere but on the gridiron, but the latter was all the coach needed or expected. And upon that very first sighting, Darrell Royal knew beyond a doubt that he wanted Earl to play for the Longhorns.

As of that evening, December 23, 1973, the recruiting for a signature of intent from Earl Campbell had officially begun.

Until that meeting, Earl had thought Ken Dabbs was the head football coach at The University of Texas, as he had spent so much time in Tyler during Earl's senior year. So he was shocked when, on the night of the state championship game, Darrell Royal was introduced to him as "the highly respected UT head coach."

Earl was once again named an All American, this time for his play at a totally different position: running back. In ten regular season high school games, he had rushed for 2,224 yards, an average of 225 yards per game — an astounding statistic considering it was only his first full year as a running back. Now he was really coming into his own. Gone was the desire to become another Dick Butkus. Earl began setting his sights on much larger goals. A college degree was hanging in the balance, if he could keep focused.

Coach La Croix once again departed from Earl's life as a coach, but the friendship was intact, and this time, Earl was mature enough to accept the loss. He vowed to never again lose his edge.

With the recruiting war beginning to escalate, Coach Nelson paid a visit to Ann Campbell to offer his expertise, since many of the recruiters began by calling on him first. He told Ann and Earl that virtually every major school in the land was aware of Earl's football abilities and would surely relish the rights to the budding superstar. Because of this, Nelson thought it imperative that the family keep the list short, considering only "core" schools relatively close to home. Ann Campbell agreed with Coach Nelson, having already decided that she didn't want "her rock" going far from the family. They agreed to shorten the list to five schools, all of them having an affiliation with the Southwest Conference: Houston, Oklahoma, Arkansas, Baylor, and The University of Texas. Recruiters from these schools were made aware of Earl's interest in them, and immediately they set out to pay him homage, laying the groundwork for "closing the deal."

As Earl was now officially eligible for recruiting, Ken Dabbs virtually moved to Tyler, at Darrell Royal's insistence. He spent seventeen consecutive days at the local Ramada Inn, each day driving to Ann Campbell's home to talk and visit. He realized that signing Earl would be a triumph for him as a recruiter. This was his first position recruiting for a legend, and Dabbs knew that Royal, already the coach of three national championship teams, expected the best. Dabbs intended to deliver. He considered Earl to be the most dominating high school football player he'd ever seen in all his years of coaching.

Ultimately Royal would also be called upon to sell Earl and Ann Campbell on the virtues of playing for The University of Texas, but, until such time as was appropriate for him to visit the Campbells, Ken Dabbs was to lay the initial groundwork. He had his work cut out for him. He would be going up against four other football powers, including Oklahoma Coach Barry Switzer, who was also chomping at the bit to sign Earl.

Dabbs explained to Earl that Darrell Royal's style of football would suit him well, and that the Longhorns genuinely needed Earl in the running back position. Royal's rushing offensive was known as "three yards and a cloud of dust," meaning the team almost always ran the ball. For a running back, this philosophy had more promise than playing for a school that depended on the passing game. Royal's dislike for the passing game is illustrated by his famous remark: "When a team throws a forward pass, three things can happen and two of them are bad."

The Tyler Rose: The Earl Campbell Story

Campbell's talents were ideal for the wishbone offense mounted by Texas, Oklahoma, or Arkansas, and all three major football powerhouses knew it. That's why Coach Royal sent Dabbs to Tyler on a full-time basis. It was a shrewd move, as none of the other schools were willing to make this commitment. Dabbs' politeness won the Campbells over, and they soon began to accept him into their lives. His undying commitment, not only to the signing of Earl Campbell, but to the entire Campbell family as well — became a distinct advantage for Texas. It was obvious that the love of the entire family would come as part of the Earl Campbell package. No other school realized or acknowledged this, a factor that didn't go unnoticed by the matriarch of the family, Ann Campbell.

By becoming close to the Campbell family, Dabbs gained valuable insight into the type of man Earl was. He learned that Earl was a quiet, intense person, with many pent-up emotions. Earl Campbell was also a lonely man, even in the midst of this huge family. Dabbs saw this loneliness in Earl's eyes. He came to understand exactly how the early death of Earl's father had affected him. He saw how Earl's abilities on the football field had grown from his need to prove himself. And he saw the anger in Earl — anger that, fortunately, was spent on the football field.

Dabbs also learned about Earl's unique connection with La Croix and what an excellent job the coach had done keeping the boy focused. Between the role model, good-guy coaching of La Croix and the disciplined, no-nonsense approach of Coach Nelson, Earl was now mentally as well as physically prepared to play for a major college football team. Dabbs made a point of getting to know both La Croix and Nelson quite well; this would streamline the process of capturing Earl's signature on a letter of intent.

Before that letter was signed, however, both Earl and Momma Campbell would have to undergo face-to-face visits with some very aggressive personalities. These recruiters would come from many miles away to sell the virtues of their programs, and each requested that the young man pay a personal visit to their campus. Each hoped they would find the correct way to approach Ann about the subject of taking her "rock" away.

Coach Dabbs certainly had done an excellent job laying the groundwork for Darrell Royal. Even so, the visit of such a well-known person created a rather awkward situation for Ann, as she has always had an enormous amount of pride in herself and her family. She was painfully aware that, no matter how much love there was inside her home, and no matter how clean she kept it, it was not a thing of beauty from the outside. Certainly it was not nearly as nice as what these coaches were accustomed to.

It worried her so much that she became ill when Darrell Royal finally came to see her, and she was forced to meet with him inside the confines of her small bedroom. If Ann was tense, so was Coach Royal, but for a different reason. His visit to Ann came on the heels of her meeting with Coach Switzer just a few days earlier, and Switzer had done an admirable job selling the virtues of attending Oklahoma. He'd even received a commitment from Earl for an upcoming visit to the school, a promise the young man fully intended to keep.

To add to the underlying tension in meeting Darrell Royal, there were the rumors that were floating around about him during this time. The scuttlebutt among most of Earl's black friends, including Reuna, was that Coach Royal was a racist. It was said that Royal was someone who was having a difficult time dealing with the influx of black players into his program. Reuna, in particular, was concerned about how Earl himself was going to react if the allegations were true. Fortunately, as Earl soon found out, these rumors were unsubstantiated. Royal was a good man as well as a good coach, and had become stereotyped by this misrepresentation. But for the time being, Earl thought it best not to tell his mother about the rumors.

When Royal arrived at Ann's home, she opened the conversation with an apology, saying she was "somewhat embarrassed" by the appearance of her house. Royal immediately put Ann at ease. He told her that he had also grown up poor — dirt poor — during the depression years in Oklahoma, raised by his grandmother without parental role models. Matter of fact, he admitted to Ann, her house was much nicer and had more furniture than the one in which he had been raised.

Then he got down to the nitty-gritty. He explained to her, in very simple terms, about the deal he was offering for her son, and what was in it for Earl. He said exactly what Ann wanted to hear. The only promise he made to her was, "If Earl works hard, *real hard*, he will walk away from The University of Texas with something more than four years of football under his belt; he'll have a college degree." He spoke smoothly to Ann, reassuring her that "Earl will be good for Texas, just as Texas will be good for Earl. What he will get is my personal concern for his well-being *and an education.* Nothing more, nothing less!"

And that was it. No more additional "perks" to try to sway the wise mother of eleven, no hidden agendas with secret "gifts" coming Earl's way. It was a remarkable sales effort, and when Darrell Royal finished speaking, he had won a large vote of confidence in the mind of Ann Campbell.

Earl, however, had yet to speak. The voices of his friends, and the lingering doubts about the rumors, still confused him.

When Earl did finally speak, it was short and to the point. "All I got to say, Coach Royal, is this: I hope you don't think Earl Campbell is for sale, 'cause I'm not. My people were bought and sold when they didn't have a choice, and I just wanted you to know that *I'M NOT FOR SALE.*"

At that moment, Darrell Royal developed an even greater appreciation for Earl Campbell, "The Man," not just the football player. His response was as simple and forthright as Earl's, "Earl, it sounds like you're the kind of man I'd like to sit down and talk with!" And before leaving, both Royal and Dabbs received a verbal commitment from Earl for a personal visit to the UT campus.

Even though Ann Campbell knew that the ultimate decision would be Earl's, she also knew in her heart where she hoped he would go. Austin, after all, was a mere four-hour drive from her home, and she didn't want Earl traveling too far from his family.

Over the course of the next week, Earl and Ann met with representatives and coaches from Arkansas, Baylor, and the University of Houston. Earl gave verbal agreements to visit Baylor and Houston. Arkansas was dropped from the list only because of its greater distance from Tyler; the decision had absolutely nothing to do with their excellent football program.

When the time came for Earl to visit the universities, he began with The University of Texas. The flight to Austin was to be Earl's first experience on an airplane, but Coach Dabbs planned to fly there and back with the novice traveler, hoping to calm any fears he might develop.

Dabbs proudly proclaims that he never committed any recruiting violations with Earl. The closest he ever came was on the flight from Tyler to Austin, when the young man was so nervous he "borrowed" some of Dabbs' Red Man chewing tobacco.

Earl could hardly be blamed for being nervous. This initial trip to Austin represented many firsts for him, beyond the fact that it was his first time on a plane. It was, for example, the first time in his life that people outside of Tyler were paying attention to him. His reception at UT marked the first time he was given the red carpet treatment, recognized by staff and team alike for his superior abilities and advanced skills.

Raymond Clayborn, a future superb NFL defensive back, met Earl at the airport. Clayborn was an easygoing student with an upbeat personality. He came across to Earl as a positive person, about himself and especially about the football program he was promoting. At this very first meeting, Clayborn told Earl that he had "definite qualities it takes to win the Heisman Trophy."

That comment didn't quite have the impact Clayborn had intended, for frankly, Earl had never even heard of the Heisman Trophy at that point in his life. All he knew were roses, Reuna, his family, the city of Tyler, and football — not necessarily in that order. Even so, the two had a great weekend together, visiting the athletic facilities, touring the campus, and meeting with Coach Royal.

As a result, Earl thought that Raymond Clayborn was "cool," and The University of Texas was "a beautiful institution." He was so pleased with his first trip away from home that during the return trip to Tyler, Earl did something totally uncharacteristic: he gave Coach Dabbs his verbal commitment to attend Texas, without first conferring with his mother about his decision. But he also told Dabbs that he was going to honor his word to Barry Switzer, and to Baylor and the University of Houston, by personally visiting their campuses. This worried Dabbs, as he was well aware that a verbal commitment was nothing without a signature on a letter of intent. He was understandably concerned, for at that point he firmly believed they would lose Earl to Oklahoma, once he visited there.

Apparently Coach Dabbs still didn't really know the heart of Earl Campbell, didn't quite understand that Earl's word, whether verbal or written, was as good as gold. If Earl gave a promise of *any* kind, it was a done deal.

Even if Dabbs had been aware of this, he still had reason for concern about Earl's upcoming trip. He knew that Oklahoma wasn't too far away from Tyler, so distance was not an issue — and a fast-talking, smooth selling recruiter or coach could easily overcome any other obstacle. Unknown to everyone, including Earl at the time, God would become the ultimate decision maker. With very little time left until the signing deadline, Earl chose to leave this enormous decision in the hands of his Higher Power — in a most interesting way.

After all the cards were on the table, played by each of the various schools, the young man still found himself in quite a dilemma. Oklahoma certainly painted a bright picture; they were first-class in their promotion, with all the players and coaches showing great optimism for Earl. Baylor and the University of Houston had been ruled out, but there were still those Sooners to contend with.

On the eve of the final day for letters of intent to be signed, and with a very troubled mind, Earl decided to do what B.C. would have done in this situation: "Pray."

His prayer was, to put it mildly, unique. It was definitely one to attract God's interest on that particular night. When Earl went to bed that evening, he silently prayed, "God, if it's your will that I should attend The University of Texas, then I'll get up during the night to pee. If not, if I sleep through the night, then I'll know your choice for me will be the University of Oklahoma."

Many years later, when Barry Switzer was informed of how Earl had ultimately decided on The University of Texas, he shook his head and said, "If I'd of known that, I'd of flown to Tyler and laid underneath his bed all night!" It didn't require divine revelation for the coach to figure out exactly what the results of his losing Earl Campbell would be: a nightmare for him each time the two schools met on the football field.

So in the end, Earl's decision to attend The University of Texas was the work of God, coming through prayer and his urinary tract. Darrell Royal was to inherit one of the greatest players he'd ever coached, by way of an emptied bladder — and he was darn proud of it.

Everyone at The University of Texas breathed a huge sigh of relief on the day the letter of intent was formally signed. Upon signing, Earl immediately claimed his famous number 20, the same one he had worn in high school, and the only number in the history of The University of Texas to ever be retired.

Earl had learned much in a three-month span, and now he had just two months left before he'd be making the biggest move of his life. He was excited about the opportunities that lay ahead. While he hoped to make Ann Campbell proud by getting a college degree, he also knew he would have an opportunity to display his athletic abilities to a hungry nation of football fanatics. And perhaps, just perhaps, he would have the chance to play professional football.

Despite the excitement, leaving home was a traumatic experience for Earl and the entire Campbell family. He would be bidding farewell to many good friends. He was leaving behind all the people he cared for — not only his family, but also Lawrence and Ann La Croix, and, of course, Reuna, who would be seeing her "hero" really leave home for the first time. Much as she would miss him, Reuna had decided to stay in Tyler and study for a nursing degree.

And then there was Corky Nelson, whose lessons in discipline had been so instrumental to Earl in his dealings with the numerous recruiters, and for whom Earl felt such deep gratitude. Nelson's disciplined style of football remained with Earl throughout his career.

Most significantly, Earl would be saying good-bye to Momma Campbell and all his family. He made many silent promises to take care of them once he became a success in college. He knew that he would one day return to his mother and family to show his gratitude for all they had done for him. As Ann La Croix had once said, Earl was a visionary.

So much was happening at once; there were so many people to say goodbye to, and, as usual, Earl found himself having a hard time verbalizing the love and sadness he was feeling.

The day before Earl departed for Austin, Ann Campbell had a conversation with Ken Dabbs, who was now a successful and highly regarded first-year recruiter. In many aspects this meeting would be a preface to the relationship these two very different people would continue to enjoy for years to come, with Earl as their common bond.

As was Ann's nature, she didn't mince any words when addressing her new friend. "Coach Dabbs, I just want you to know that I'm holdin' you personally responsible for my Earl. While he's there in Austin, you watch over my rock, and be sure no harm comes to him, and I'll always be grateful that you came through on our agreement."

Dabbs knew exactly what Ann meant. He looked forward to protecting the well-being of the future Heisman Trophy winner.

Earl stopped working in the rose fields the summer after his high school graduation, vowing never to go back again. He had finally accepted the gift that God had given him, and he fully intended to acknowledge His blessing while attending The University of Texas.

Although Earl would be leaving Tyler that year, perhaps for good, he would never allow the memories, good or bad, to leave him. A city of people had embraced him, without regard to the color of his skin. From now on, wherever he was in *his* life, Earl Campbell would always be a bright spot in theirs.

He truly had become their "Tyler Rose."

SECTION III

HOOK 'EM HORNS

THE EYES OF TEXAS
ARE UPON YOU

The eyes of Texas are upon you
All the livelong day
The eyes of Texas are upon you
You cannot get away
Do not think you can escape them
At night or early in the morn
The eyes of Texas are upon you
'Til Gabriel blows his horn.

Sing me a song of prexy
Of days long since gone by
Again I sing to greet him
And hear his kind reply
Smiles of gracious welcome
Before my memory rise
Again I hear him say to me
Remember Texas' eyes.

"Earl Campbell is a good man. He cares for all people, with no barriers surrounding them. He gives more to people today than he ever gave on a football field and, believe me, he gave his all on a football field."

Darrell Royal, Coach
The University of Texas, 1957-1976

The main campus of The University of Texas at Austin is an ominous sight, especially for a young man who has spent his entire life in deep East Texas. Tyler, Swann, and the surrounding countryside would seem like the end of the earth to most Austin aristocrat types.

Earl arrived at UT his first day with only one pair of jeans, a pair of cut-offs, several T-shirts, one suit (which Reuna had made for their senior prom), and forty dollars. The forty dollars was perhaps the most money he had ever had in his pocket at any one time, and Earl believed he was "nothing short of rich."

Earl had been awestruck when he first visited UT during recruitment, but as he walked the wide lawns of the sprawling campus, he was overwhelmed. He was overwhelmed not only by the size of the place, but by his very decision to come to UT. Here he was, a black kid from East Texas, looking up at the high old windows of the academic halls. He was frightened. But, he reminded himself, he was also The Tyler Rose, the best football recruit to come from *anywhere*. He straightened his shoulders and ran up the steps to Jester Hall, the multi-floored dorm that would be his home in Austin for the next three years.

Located squarely in the heart of downtown Austin, the campus took up an area that, according to Earl, appeared "bigger than the entire city of Tyler." In fact, he wasn't far off. The student population of the school includes upwards of 50,000 degree-bound individuals at any given time. Comprised of 357 acres and 120 large buildings, the campus is centered around the infamous Tower. The Tower is the magnetic hub of the campus universe. Its top floors are awash in an orange glow after every football victory, and, in the best old Southwest Conference tradition, the entire building blazes orange after any victory over the Aggies, or after winning a national championship. Earl had, indeed, entered a "city within a city."

Earl realized on the very first day that his time at UT wasn't to be a "vacation" such as he'd experienced during the past summer on his recruiting trip. No, this was of far greater importance. He understood that this first day at The University of Texas was literally the beginning of a new life. In this new life, Earl would come to realize total maturity and manhood under the auspices of many new leaders, several of whom he would admire and emulate beyond his years spent at The University of Texas.

Although he was awed by the size of the campus and the

magnitude of the dreams he held, Earl vowed on that very first day in Austin that he wouldn't be intimidated by anything or anyone. This vow was forged by his hunger to excel in both his studies and football, and tempered by his desire to never go back to the poverty he had left behind in Tyler. He was on a mission to prove those people wrong who had him stereotyped as just another "stupid jock."

The stupid-jock nametag was brought to his attention at the Longhorns' first practice as he was running around the track, loosening up for the workout ahead. Louis Murillo, a 5'2" Mexican-American ball of dynamite who had worked in The University of Texas Athletic Department for twenty-two years, began walking across the field for his first encounter with the new recruit. It was apparent by the pace of Murillo's walk that he had something pressing on his mind, a matter he wished to get off his chest, "up front" with this enormous black man. Darrell Royal had made Murillo aware of Earl Campbell's presence only several minutes earlier, prompting what would be a most important meeting.

When Earl noticed the diminutive man walking directly toward him he stopped, curious. What Murillo had to say was simple and to the point. "Mr. Campbell, I'm Louis Murillo. I just wanted you to know that you're not gonna be just another dumb nigger who plays four years of football and then leaves without a degree. *I'm gonna see to that!*"

Obviously, this first encounter with Murillo could have gone in several different directions, most leading to the immediate demise of the brave — but much smaller — man. Indeed, in any other scenario, someone addressing the massive gridiron star the way Murillo did may well have had his teeth handed back to him. Instead, Earl weighed Murillo's words, and realized that this small man was giving him a large dose of wisdom. Truth be told, Murillo's blunt message epitomized what Earl himself had been feeling since his arrival a few days earlier. So he let the words pass for what they were, "a lesson," and then put Murillo's mind at ease by shaking his hand in appreciation for his courage. This was, after all, a case of one minority candidly addressing another, about a phenomenon he had witnessed as the norm for most black athletes.

Unfortunate as it was, most minority athletes did their time in their sport, then left school with nothing to show for it. They left with no professional contract to negotiate and, more importantly to Murillo as well as to Earl, no college degree for security in a world without football. Murillo took a genuine interest in Earl — not only in what he could do for The University of Texas on a football field, but in the young man himself. He truly wanted Earl to leave the school with more than memories of glory and a beaten and bruised body. It was for this reason, after Earl fully evaluated what Murillo had said to him, that the two men soon became the best of friends. From that first meeting, Louis Murillo was a valued adviser and confidante to the young athlete, and would remain so for many years.

God saw to it that Louis Murillo's lesson wasn't lost on Earl.

The University of Texas, like the state itself, is steeped in tradition. Most of the school's tradition stems from its football program, dating back to the first team that was fielded in 1893, when UT defeated the Dallas Football Club, 18-16. In that first season, Texas had a mere fifteen players on their roster and finished the year 4-0. The precedent and motto for every Longhorn team to follow was established: "Losing is not an option." Through the years, football and winning became synonymous at this famed institution. Each passing year produced yet another chapter for the statisticians and glorified alumni to follow with religious fervor.

With all the magnificent teams that this proud university has produced, none would be more significant to the American public than those coached by the legend, Darrell Royal, or *"The Coach,"* as he would come to be known. Never before and never since has one man had such an impact — not just on a single institution, but on an entire nation of football followers. Never before or since has one man been as capable of silencing an audience, simply with his presence. Royal's three national championships propelled him to legendary status in the eyes of a core of fanatics who equated Longhorn football dominance to collegiate superiority. There simply was no substitute for victory, nor any logical justification for defeat.

Such was the environment Earl Campbell encountered as he donned the burnt orange and white of Texas.

Little could Earl have known at the time that his freshman class would be the last major recruiting *coup* for Coach Royal. Toward the end of his tenure, Royal became increasingly disgruntled by the amount of cheating that was occurring at other institutions. He found it ever more difficult to ethically capture many of the "blue chip" prospects that Texas' high schools produced each year. As each new season approached, Royal would see these young men going elsewhere, many times outside the state. These vulnerable recruits were lured by the promise of cash and other under-the-table amenities. Because of this alarming increase in recruiting chicanery, the freshman class of '74 at The University of Texas is considered by many historians to be the last bastion of Coach Royal's recruiting dominance in the South.

Darrell Royal was definitely bucking the tide. Even to the very end he had one rule by which he insisted all his recruiters abide: "We will not coerce a young man by promises of anything more than a scholarship and, if he works hard, a degree. Above all else, *our* integrity must remain intact when dealing with these young men and their families, so we'll never have to hang our heads in shame."

It was this simple rule, and Coach Royal's inherent integrity, that enabled him to sign young men the likes of Earl Campbell, Alfred Jackson, Rick Ingraham, and Brad Shearer (the future Outland Trophy winner). Elsewhere, cheating was widespread and blatant, and the face of college football was changing dramatically amid outlandish recruiting promises and flagrant violations.

As Coach Royal headed into the '74 season, the main thing that he had going in his favor was a relatively new rule that freshmen were now eligible to play on the varsity level. This rule made it possible for an athlete such as Earl Campbell to display his many talents to an entire nation of followers. Although athletic scholarships were now limited to thirty per year, the freshman eligibility rule would allow Coach Royal to bring these novice collegiate players along, at a proper pace, on the varsity level. This enabled Royal to prepare these young men for what would be expected of them when their recruiting class had come full circle, at which time *they* would be looked upon to carry the mystique of Longhorn football forward.

As Earl Campbell prepared for his freshman year of eligibility, he was hoping desperately that he would be able to properly inter-mingle his studies with the enormous strain of playing high-visibility college football. Earl was fully aware that he would carry this double burden with him as his career progressed. What he didn't know yet, but would be forced to learn quickly, was that he was being looked upon to be *the* future of Longhorn football. This high-visibility image meant that much more than just his football talents and accomplish-ments were to be showcased at UT.

It wasn't too long before he figured out that his professors and fellow classmates were watching closely to see if, in fact, Earl Campbell fit the stereotype of "the stupid jock." They checked to see if he attended classes and if he paid attention and participated. And so, beginning with his first semester classes, Earl knew that he would have to accept the spotlight and carry this additional burden. For him there was only one logical way to handle this. He made a decision on the first day of classes "to attend *every* class and sit in the very first row." If his enormous size and reputation made it inevitable that The Eyes of Texas would be upon him for more than his ability to score touchdowns, then he might as well meet the challenge head-on. It was, after all, the way he'd met all his previous challenges. Earl Campbell made up his mind that he was going to defeat this "dumb jock syndrome" with any and all resources that were available.

Sitting in the first row at every class was a good beginning. Realizing that it would take more than appearances to get him through school, however, Earl utilized another resource at hand: John Pinto, a student tutor. As Louis Murillo had done, Pinto took a keen interest in Earl's college career. He had tutored many athletes in the past, but Earl was different. Earl possessed a unique quality that wasn't often seen in athletes: the desire to succeed, no matter what the costs.

As Earl realized over the course of his college years, these costs would oftentimes be extreme when combined with a grueling football schedule, but the reward would be well worth his determined effort.

Earl Campbell played his first collegiate game at Boston College on September 14, 1974. Although he was nervous, especially since the team had to fly to this first important meeting, Earl didn't openly display any jitters once he was on the field. He rushed for 85 yards on 13 carries in a 42-19 Longhorn thrashing of their gracious host from Massachusetts. And yet, although the team won handily, Earl wasn't satisfied with his performance. Earl was *never* satisfied in his quest for success. Regardless, he did appreciate the camaraderie that accompanied this road victory during the return flight to Austin. It was this fellowship that made away games much more fun for Earl than home games.

As the Longhorns began practice for their home opener against the Wyoming Cowboys on September 21st, Earl had to prepare for more than the wishbone offense that he was working so diligently to comprehend. He was fortunate that there were veteran players such as Roosevelt Leaks and Raymond Clayborn to take him under their wing. Leaks, who quietly symbolized the emergence of black athletes into the mainstream of Texas Longhorn sports, combined his knowledge with the inherent leadership abilities of Clayborn. Together they worked to get the newcomer mentally prepared for the home opener at Memorial Stadium, the home field for Longhorn football. Though Earl had played before large hometown crowds while attending John Tyler High School, and at the state championship game in the Astrodome, Leaks and Clayborn tried to impress upon him that "there's really nothing that can prepare you for the sea of burnt orange and white you'll encounter, once you walk out onto that field."

During practice, Earl would often look around the stadium, which was capable of holding 75,000 spectators, and he'd think to himself, "There's no way they'll fill this place. No way, man!"

The mental preparation that Leaks and Clayborn had been putting the freshmen through helped Earl begin to visualize actually playing the games. He tried to place himself on the field in game situations, and to prepare for the crowd and the tumultuous noise that would penetrate his entire being. Still, as he had been told, no one — not Roosevelt Leaks, not Raymond Clayborn, not even Darrell Royal himself — could truly prepare Earl for what he encountered that first hot, sunny afternoon in Austin, Texas.

As most teams do, the Longhorns had a team breakfast before departing for Memorial Stadium to get taped and to go through their pregame drills. Kickoff was set for 1:00 P.M. All morning, a nervous knot had been forming inside Earl's stomach, and even the memory of the 'Horns' opening game victory did little to abate his nervousness. He tried repeatedly to reassure himself, especially beginning around 11:30, when the spectators started trickling into the stadium.

"Nothin' major," he reasoned. "I *know* they'll never fill this stadium, especially that huge upper deck." The upper deck Earl referred to is a seemingly endless formation of seats on the home side of the field. Soaring skyward, these stadium seats are clearly visible to people traveling on Interstate 35, a major thoroughfare cutting through

Austin. And so far they were virtually empty.

Very soon, however, Earl would find himself having to eat his words about those seats. By 12:30, both teams had aborted their drills and entered their respective locker rooms to put full pads on in preparation for the pre-game lineup introductions. Earl knelt on one knee and listened to Coach Royal give last minute instructions. The coach spoke to his team of the "pride that it takes to become true *winners* for The University of Texas."

As Coach Royal spoke, Earl began to hear the noise emanating from what he still believed to be a half-filled stadium. When the team exited the locker room and headed down the runway leading to the stadium floor, they encountered grown men, women, and little children in a line formation that they were forced to follow. These spectators were desperately trying to touch the players, their shoulder pads, or any portion of their uniforms. Just in case there'd been any doubt, their screams brought it home to the team that "The Eyes of Texas" were definitely upon them.

When Earl finally hit daylight and the entrance to the field, he was downright dazed by what he saw. The stadium definitely did not appear as it had just one brief hour earlier. There before him, in all their glory, were over 75,000 people. The majority of the fans were dressed in burnt orange and white, reflecting the proud tradition of the Texas Longhorns. The home field side, including the enormous upper deck, consisted of The University of Texas Alumni, while the visitors' side held the active Texas students. The few fans from Wyoming who had made the nearly-thousand-mile journey deep into the heart of Texas were located in a corner of the south end zone.

Earl stared, flabbergasted, as the knot that was already present in his stomach grew to basketball-size proportions. He suddenly felt a desperate need to hit someone, or be hit by someone, in order to rid himself of the feeling that had suddenly descended upon him. Earl notes, "In all my years playin' football, I'd *never* felt like that before."

Hook 'Em 'Horns

Exacerbating the nervous tension that seized him was the sound of The University of Texas Marching Band. Their repeated playing of the Texas Fight Song only helped enhance the fans' frenzied state. Earl could do little more than stare in amazement as the combined noise of the crowd and band became, as he describes it, "a mere echo" in his head. Everything seemed a little bit unreal to him. Even the incessant pounding of "Big Bertha" — the band's enormous bass drum measuring 54 inches around and weighing over 500 pounds — wasn't quite registering in Earl's brain. All he could concentrate on was "takin' the first lick" so that he could rid himself of whatever had taken hold of his mental framework. After what seemed like hours, the starting offensive team for the Longhorns was introduced, and the remainder of the team took the field, fully prepared for the battle that was about to ensue.

Although he didn't start that home-opening game, Earl did finally get rid of the nervousness with his first run — and then he rushed 10 times for 85 yards, with his longest run being 13 yards. But something even more significant happened during this game, and it proved to be an omen to Longhorn fans in the future: Earl Campbell scored his first touchdown for the burnt orange and white.

The 'Horns easily defeated Wyoming, 34-7, and young Earl Campbell had to face his first "media circus" after the game. This public display was something he was neither good at nor prepared for.

After the press conference, he gratefully retreated to Jester Hall with Reuna, who came to all the home games during Earl's UT career. Aside from her cheerful disposition, which Earl desperately depended on, Reuna brought news about his family, Coach and Ann La Croix, and all his close friends in Tyler. She also brought care packages to Earl, filled with food, clothing, and personal items to further emphasize the still blossoming affection she held for her hero. Reuna knew, better than everyone else, that Earl was lonely and homesick in Austin without his family and her to comfort him. She listened to Earl talk about his desolation after the games, when he found himself most in need of those people he missed.

Earl had no money, and really had nowhere else to go after a game except back to the dormitory. It was here that he would try to adjust to the sudden contrast between 75,000 screaming fans and the ensuing solitude. Reuna helped assuage his loneliness for awhile, but he was always painfully aware that she would eventually have to leave for her four-hour drive back to Tyler. And once she was gone, the acute feeling of sadness would become all-encompassing. This was a feeling Earl would experience many times in the future, and one he would come to despise. After these home games, in the solitude that followed Reuna's departure, Earl learned to truly appreciate their friendship. It was here, in this self-imposed seclusion, that he came to know how important her presence was in his life.

With the win against Wyoming behind them, the Longhorns were ranked sixth in the nation. Naturally, this was quite a feeling for a young man only two months into his freshman year. Earl had finally exorcised the nervous demons from his body, and now the team was preparing for their first Southwest Conference game. This would be a major test, as they would be traveling to Lubbock to play the Red Raiders of Texas Tech. Although the first two games had been won handily by the Longhorns, inter-conference games were always played with a fevered intensity, because bitter conference rivalries had developed over the years. UT and Texas Tech shared one of these rivalries.

Even though he had played only sporadically during the first two games, Earl was beginning to feel, ever more acutely, that inner need to excel. Earl always expected much more from himself than the spectators did, and his heightened expectations became the measuring stick by which he evaluated his performances. But he drew on the strength of his audience too. After scoring his first touchdown against Wyoming, the Tyler Rose felt the immense strength and power derived from the spectators. This only served to reinforce his personal goal of offering and delivering "a hundred times more than *they* expect of me." Earl Campbell was never satisfied with his performance, *ever*. He knew that being merely satisfied with his abilities would mean that he was no longer "hungry" for victory — and hungry for victory was how he intended to remain for the duration of his career.

The trip to Texas Tech marked Earl's first visit to Lubbock. Flying into this sparsely populated west Texas city fascinated him as he gazed upon the countless oil wells dotting the flat farmland of the Southern Panhandle. This game would be significant to Earl, for it marked his first taste of defeat as a Longhorn — a humiliating 26-3 loss to the unranked Red Raiders.

Coach Royal increased Earl's playing time during this game, allowing him to carry the ball 16 times. Unfortunately, the Tech defense was up to the challenge as they held the future star to a mere 52 yards. The Tech defense managed to do something that no other team had ever done to Earl Campbell, up to that point: hold him to an average of only 3.25 yards rushing. Tech had a swarming defense that dealt many punishing blows, not only to Earl, but to the entire Longhorn team. Earl would not experience the thrill of another touchdown in this game, and the 'Horns had to face the reality of a resounding defeat.

In the locker room, Coach Royal advised his warriors: "True winners learn to accept defeat as well as victory, and to deal with defeat in an appropriate manner." For Earl, it was a bitter pill to swallow, since it was the first time in over two years that he had to accept the sting of losing.

After the game, on the flight to Austin, a somewhat subdued Tyler Rose evaluated his weak performance, and re-confirmed two obvious certainties: he'd much rather win than lose, and he'd much rather hit than be hit. These became Earl's credo. Actually living up to his credo was the difficult part, now that he was truly in the ranks of "big time college football."

Though Darrell Royal appreciated the victories that his team provided for him and the school, he understood that his main priority as a coach was to "get the players through their years, hopefully, with a degree in hand." It was with this philosophy in mind that he and his staff continually monitored his players' grades. Royal held firm to the essence of his recruiting pitch that "if you work hard, you'll also walk away with a degree."

During his first semester at school, Earl took only the basic required courses, because he hadn't the faintest idea of what he wished to major in or what he wanted to do in life. In reality, sticking to these basic courses worked to his advantage, as Earl knew that his first semester would be the hardest. He still adhered to his rule to attend every class, every day, sitting in the first row so that the teachers and students would be aware of his presence.

Rick Ingraham, Earl's teammate during the four years he played at The University of Texas, best summarized Earl's desire to acquire his college degree: "Earl may not have been the best or brightest student who attended Texas, but he was definitely a serious student!"

After only three games, Coach Royal was well aware that Earl Campbell would have a huge impact on Texas football. He only hoped God would see to it that the young man remained healthy. Darrell Royal had been in football long enough to know a future star when he saw one, and when he looked at Earl, he knew this young man was destined for greatness in the National Football League. In fact, Royal had sensed Earl's destiny the first time he'd witnessed the young man play. "*That's* how good Earl was," Royal says.

These accolades are not to be taken lightly, coming from a man who became a living legend while coaching at Texas, a man who had witnessed many other fine ballplayers before Earl Campbell. It has never been Royal's style to make extravagant statements.

Whatever the future would bring for Earl Campbell, Royal knew that his own immediate future, with Earl Campbell in his backfield, would bring an unprecedented string of victories for the 'Horns.

After their resounding defeat by Texas Tech, the Longhorns prepared to play the University of Washington. UT had dropped from sixth to seventh place in the national rankings. The players realized that this next game would be pivotal in determining their standing, as the remainder of their schedule consisted of the six Southwest Conference opponents, plus Oklahoma University.

The Oklahoma game was scheduled for the following week in the Cotton Bowl. Coach Royal tried to get the team to focus only on the game with unranked Washington — which was somewhat of a challenge because his teams tended to look ahead rather than to the task at hand. In this case they were looking ahead to the Oklahoma game, an annual competitive ritual that excited the entire campus. Coach Royal had his work cut out for him in trying to keep the team centered on the upcoming face-off with Washington.

The fans, however, certainly had no trouble focusing on the Washington game; Memorial Stadium was sold out for the match. It was standing room only. This game will long be remembered by staunch Texas supporters as the first game in which Earl Campbell rushed for over a hundred yards. He gained 125 yards on 16 carries, with one touchdown in the process. It was obvious that Earl had listened to his coach, and had concentrated on the game.

His longest gain of 36 yards would prompt Louis Murillo, Earl's friend and confidante, to proudly state, "Earl Campbell has a little of Jim Brown, a little of Gayle Sayers, and a *lot* of bull in him!"

When questioned by the media after the game, Coach Royal

stated simply, "It was a fine performance by an outstanding young athlete."

As for Earl, he rarely said anything to the media, being extremely shy and not wanting to make a fool of himself. He was, however, smart enough to understand that, "once you've had a big game like I did against Washington, then the media expect you to meet or exceed [your performance in] that game as the weeks progress." Despite his naivete, the young man had pegged the reporters correctly. All he would say after that Washington game was, "thanks," even though the reporters deluged him with various compliments and tried to get him to say something, *anything,* that could be used as a quote from this newly established Longhorns star.

The week prior to the Texas-OU game creates mass hysteria for both campuses, for their alumni, and for the city of Dallas, where the Cotton Bowl is located. This annual contest is held in Dallas because it is a "neutral site," being roughly an equal distance from both campuses. Holding the game on one or the other campus would create total chaos among the avid alumni and student body fans. So the chaos was moved to Dallas, where the streets of "Big D" were literally taken over by the OU and UT fans, and painted red or orange respectively.

To add to the festive atmosphere, the elaborate Texas State Fair is held throughout the week prior to the game, on the grounds surrounding the Cotton Bowl. This allows ample opportunity for alumni and students alike to party and prepare for what is considered the Super Bowl of The Southwest.

This particular Oklahoma game would have a special significance for Earl, as it symbolized his initiation into genuine Longhorns football fanaticism. Even though he had conquered his early game jitters, especially the kind he'd experienced in the first home game, Earl was awestruck as he took to the field for this bitter rivalry. As a result of the constant schooling from Roosevelt Leaks and Raymond Clayborn, Earl was already fully aware that the Texas/Oklahoma game is played for pride, unlike the Texas/A&M game, which is played for "bragging rights" in the State of Texas.

As he surveyed the spectators, Earl was stunned by the animosity in the stadium. He remembers, "It wasn't like they hated each other, 'cause they didn't know each other personally. It was more like an anger that surfaced once a year for four hours. I mean, the people from each school were goin' berserk, forgettin' all about manners and the pleasantries usually extended to the rival team."

Earl knew that in the Texas/Oklahoma annual shootout, there was no formal "home team." Each side was allotted half the available tickets, creating a sea of red and white on one side, burnt orange and white on the other. And now Earl *was* starting to feel a bit of nervousness, much akin to what he'd experienced during his first Texas home game against Wyoming. Obscenities were raining down on Coach Royal and all the Texas players and, although he couldn't hear them, Earl was sure the same thing was happening to Barry Switzer and the Sooners.

Oklahoma had come into this Cotton Bowl ranked second in the country, with Texas holding the fifth position. As a result, this particular game would be played for far more than pride, since a first place ranking was a distinct possibility for the winner. In addition, the game was being played before a national television audience and, as all football followers — not to mention players — are aware, this type of exposure is an arena for future recruitment by the pro teams.

As the National Anthem was being played, Earl looked out over the sea of red that comprised the Oklahoma supporters, and a humorous thought crossed his mind. He realized that the State Fair, that enormous carnival going on outside the stadium, was completely overshadowed by the carnival that was happening within the confines of the Cotton Bowl.

The Tyler Rose: The Earl Campbell Story

"At least," he thought to himself, "Reuna is here to cheer me on, and all my family is gettin' to watch me play on television." Earl's musings served to distract him, at least temporarily, from the reality of playing against the feared Oklahoma Selmon brothers. But if Earl hadn't been truly aware of Leroy, Lucius, and Dewey Selmon before the game, he *became* aware the first time he carried the ball.

As in many previous games between the two bitter rivals, this one was extremely close, with fierce hitting occurring on both sides of the line. And much of the hitting on the Sooners' side came from the Brothers Selmon. Recalls Earl, "They were grown men, *big* men, and they were *mean*. Man, were they mean. They put several knots on my head that day but, don't get me wrong, many of the Oklahoma players, *includin'* the Selmon brothers, left that stadium with knots on *their* heads — knots that *I* had given *them*."

Continuing to reflect back on his first meeting against Oklahoma, Earl smiles. "Remember, those boys on the Oklahoma team had been tryin' to recruit me just the year before. Coach Switzer had gone above and beyond the call of duty tryin' to capture my services. Since I decided not to go there, I guess they all felt it was necessary to give me something' to remember them by. Likewise, I felt it was only fair to place the Longhorn brand on top of their helmets. It was a heckuva ballgame, I'll tell y'all that much!"

A "heckuva ballgame," indeed. The game was a true nail-biter that went down to the final gun with Oklahoma proudly carrying a 16-13 victory back to their campus. Although Texas lost, they did so with respectability in front of an entire viewing nation. And Earl gained national recognition in that game. He racked up 70 yards rushing on 15 attempts, scoring once in the process. After the game ended, Earl Campbell and Barry Switzer embraced at midfield, each equally aware of what the Tyler Rose could have done for the Oklahoma football program had he elected to become a Sooner.

The return trip to Austin was excruciatingly long for the

Longhorn team, with each player pondering the "what ifs." The following day Earl attended church. This was his habit every Sunday morning; he'd leave the other students sleeping or dealing with a hangover, and walk from Jester Hall to his church. He liked these peaceful Sunday mornings, when the street was quiet and devoid of rushing students. Though he was often sore and sometimes even limping from his football injuries, he always went to church. He did it out of respect for God, ever mindful of the teachings of Ann and B.C. Campbell.

He also went to church simply to give thanks for his God-given abilities. Win or lose, Earl always made sure that he thanked God because, without His many blessings, he knew that his ability to perform in the classroom and on the field would not exist.

After church and a quick bite to eat, it was off to the training room to "ice down" the many sore areas of his body. This part of his Sunday routine was particularly welcome after the punishment that the Selmon brothers had inflicted upon him. Now, at last, Earl had a chance to reflect on his performance the day before. As usual, he was critical of himself. He knew that Fred Akers, the Longhorn backfield coach, had already assessed the inefficiencies of his players from the day before, so he sought Akers out to compare game notes and to get the coach's opinion about how he could play better football.

Earl also took advantage of this slack time to wonder what his momma, his brothers and sisters, Coach La Croix, and all his friends had thought yesterday as they'd watched him perform on television. As always, when all his reflecting was finished, Earl was not satisfied. He understood that he still had a tremendous amount to learn and much to prove to himself, to his family, to his school, and to his hometown.

Fortunately for Coach Royal and the rest of the Longhorn squad, the team didn't have time to reflect on their loss to Oklahoma for very long. The following Saturday, they were scheduled to play at home against the powerful Arkansas Razorbacks. The Arkansas game would also be televised nationally, which, they hoped, would allow the Longhorns to make a better showing. They had fallen to eighth in the national rankings, quite a drop considering how close the OU game had been. They could no longer afford to look back, needing instead to prepare for the battle with another bitter rival and fellow member of the Southwest Conference.

Earl, in his finest performance to date, rushed 8 times for 109 yards, an average of a staggering 13.6 yards per carry. He also scored a touchdown in a 38-7 demolition of the Razorbacks, leaving many of their players, coaches, and faithful followers to wonder, "Who the heck was that, and where did he come from?"

In one of Coach Royal's proudest moments, Earl single-handedly destroyed the Razorback team. With only four minutes left until half-time in a scoreless game, the Razorbacks were forced to punt from deep in their own territory. Coach Royal, knowing about Earl's defensive abilities in high school, had been practicing the young man with the punting team to make him aware of what was expected in this position. Given the current situation, Coach Royal decided he needed Earl.

"Earl, I want you to get in there and block that punt," Royal commanded.

The coach wanted to see what, if anything, Earl had learned during these practice sessions. He should have known his protégé had learned plenty. Earl broke through Arkansas' line, untouched, and proceeded to block the punt into the Arkansas end zone, where it was recovered by a fellow teammate. Royal could do nothing but grin in admiration, but Earl still wasn't finished. On the very next series of plays, Arkansas was once again forced to punt, the ball coming to rest on the Longhorn 32-yard line. With only one minute left before halftime, Royal called Earl's number. Once again Earl responded, this time with a 68-yard touchdown run. From that point forward, the game was over. Earl had driven a stake into the hearts of Arkansas fans everywhere. This freshman rookie had stilled the thunder of the Razorback's rough, raw-edged "Su-wee" cry.

As was becoming customary, Earl responded to the media with one- or two-word answers, ever humble and polite. He preferred to brag on the offensive line, "who made this fine showing possible." Wisely, he still chose not to expose himself to the ever-fickle media. As he had after the hundred-plus yard game against Washington, Earl knew to keep quiet. A mediocre or poor showing the following week would leave him wide open for vicious criticism at the hands of the same writers who were trying desperately to get him to open up.

"Right or wrong," Earl reflects back on those early hundred yard performances, "I knew that keeping quiet was the best avenue to take, even though it made many reporters sore as heck at me." It was remarkable how this young man, just four months out of high school, had the presence of mind to humble himself and keep the media at bay — in marked contrast to the chest-beating prima-donnas in the supposedly "adult" NFL of today.

After the game, Earl and Reuna went back to Jester Hall as usual. Her company was all he needed to relax and be happy. During the brief periods of time they spent together, Reuna continued to brighten Earl's world with updates about his family and all that was happening in the city of Tyler.

The following week found the Longhorns, still maintaining their eighth seed in the national rankings, playing at Rice Stadium in Houston against the Owls. As was becoming commonplace, Earl ground out 105 yards on 18 carries, his longest run being a 23-yard scamper around the end. Although he didn't score a touchdown that day, the 'Horns won easily, 27-6, and Earl's reputation continued to grow, among his opponents as well as his teammates.

Respect from and for his opponents was always important to

The Tyler Rose: The Earl Campbell Story

Earl. He firmly believed that, "Those who play against you are the best critics you will find. Unlike your friends, *your opponents will always be straight with you, will always tell it like it really is!*"

Next up for the Longhorns were the Southern Methodist Mustangs. Still ranked eighth nationally, the Longhorns thrashed the Ponies at Memorial Stadium, 35-15. Earl gained 54 yards on 15 carries and added another touchdown to his impressive list of accomplishments. The media continued to hound Earl for some kind of quote or interview, but he still felt uncomfortable in front of a microphone or camera. How could he possibly flaunt his own prowess? That just wasn't his style. The few words he did mumble only praised the whole team's efforts.

After defeating SMU, the Longhorns moved up in the national rankings to number seven. Their next game was against Baylor University in Waco, Texas. It was crucial to win this game if they wished to maintain a top-ten standing. The Baylor Bears were unranked, but were determined to win on the heels of an embarrassing 42-6 defeat against the 'Horns the previous year at Memorial Stadium. Perhaps it was the Bears' staunch determination, or perhaps it was just that the Longhorns weren't mentally prepared for the game. Maybe they were too sure of themselves, and riding high on their three-game winning streak. At any rate, the Bears answered the previous year's humiliation with a beating of their own. They handed the highly ranked 'Horns an embarrassing 34-24 defeat, and an instant drop in the national rankings.

Even in defeat, Earl had rushed 83 yards on 14 carries with one touchdown. To him, however, "Statistics are bittersweet, when achieved in the arms of defeat."

Once again, the return trip to Austin was silent. The 'Horns found themselves dropping ten full points, down to seventeenth in the national placement. For a school accustomed to top national rankings, this latest demotion was a slap in the face. The team vowed vengeance against Texas Christian University the following week at a game to be played in Ft. Worth, home of the TCU Horned Frogs.

It was more than an act of vengeance when the Longhorns virtually destroyed TCU in front of their home crowd, with a final score of 81-16. The Texas team knew they had to have this type of showing to recoup the respect of those who determined the national rankings. Earl ran the ball nine times for 64 yards. Having such a margin of victory, the Longhorns found themselves with the luxury of playing many of their second and third string players for most of the second half. After the TCU game the 'Horns moved up ten places in the polls, bringing them back to number seven. And now they began preparing in earnest for their annual Thanksgiving Day game against the eighth-ranked Texas A&M Aggies.

The Texas A&M game was the first time Earl could remember being away from home on Thanksgiving Day. Thanksgiving in Tyler was a special day of visiting and eating with family and friends. In the locker room getting taped, he imagined all of the smells he remembered coming from his mother's kitchen — the fat bird, giblet gravy, and pumpkin pie. Turkey Day in his house would be different this year. He was in Austin, and his family would be watching him on national TV.

The Aggie football program is characterized by its own brand of Texas tradition, but many of these practices were unknown to Earl at the time. He didn't know that the night before their annual game against Texas, the Aggie students, alumni, and supporters attended an enormous bonfire on the A&M campus. At this bonfire, they practiced "yells," led by their many "yell leaders." Aggies *never* referred to these as cheers.

Earl also wasn't aware of the many "Aggie jokes" that had been created by UT students and alumni over the years. These Aggie jokes were clearly aimed at making fun of students and graduates of Texas A&M University. That fall, Earl heard his first Aggie joke and learned about the animosity that the schools held toward each other when playing football, an animosity that lingers even today.

Earl was surprised when he took to the field for this home game and saw the throngs of Aggie supporters, not to mention the famous Aggie band. "Odd," he thought to himself. "In all our other home games, there weren't near this many fans from the other team. How in the world did A&M manage to pull this off?"

The answer, of course, lay in the proximity of the two campuses. College Station is a mere ninety-minute drive from Austin — two hours max, depending on how much liquid refreshment might be consumed in preparation for this yearly battle for Texas bragging rights.

To Earl, it seemed that spectators from both sides had ingested more beer than turkey in preparation for the showdown. Unfortunately for the Aggies and their supporters, however, the Longhorns were running on all cylinders as they handed A&M a devastating 32-3 defeat in this last regular season game. Earl had a career high day, gaining 127 yards on 28 carries. The Aggies lost their top-ten national ranking, but gained a great respect for the player who had wreaked havoc on their defense. As for Earl, all he could say to the media hounding him for a quote was, "Thanks, I owe it all to our offensive line," thereby frustrating their hunger for a new sports celebrity once again.

The Longhorns' two Southwest Conference losses kept them from going to the Cotton Bowl that year. Instead, they settled for a Gator Bowl invitation, where Auburn soundly defeated them, 27-3. Earl failed to achieve his personal goal of a thousand-yard rushing season, settling for 928 yards over the course of the regular ten-game season. Even so, these numbers were good enough to get him voted Southwest Conference Newcomer of the Year, an honor bestowed upon him by the coaches for those teams he played against.

Characteristically, however, he remained dissatisfied with his performance, for it didn't measure up to *his* standards. The disappointing season finale against Auburn did nothing more than fan the fire that had been burning in Earl's gut. What he really wanted was to be in the starting offensive lineup *and* gain over a thousand yards his sophomore year. It was with this flame roaring inside him that Earl set about preparing for the next season, and his preparation began immediately after the Auburn game.

With the help of John Pinto, his tutor and friend, Earl passed all of his courses with a C average the first half of his freshman year. He also obtained some much-needed direction from Roosevelt Leaks, who suggested that Earl try speech classes in his second semester. Earl did so, and liked the classes and teachers so much that he decided to major in Speech Communications. He thoroughly enjoyed the various speeches he had to prepare and recite in class. He also realized that these speech courses would better prepare him for dealing with the media, who were anxiously awaiting the moment when Earl Campbell would utter more than one or two mumbled words.

In many instances, it wasn't that he didn't want to talk, but rather that he simply didn't know what to say. Above all, he didn't want to jeopardize his image or that of his team by saying the wrong thing at the wrong time. Earl decided that a degree in Speech would give him the self-confidence to present himself as the star that he was.

As preparation for the '75 season began, Earl found himself more focused than he had ever been before, both scholastically and athletically. He vowed to stop at nothing to ensure that his name would appear in the starting backfield on the 'Horns weekly depth chart. And he was still determined to meet his personal goal of gaining a thousand yards in the season.

The Tyler Rose: The Earl Campbell Story

The media had become less enamored of Coach Royal because of his failure to claim another Southwest Conference championship, not to mention the embarrassing year-ending defeat at the hands of Auburn. Earl liked Darrell Royal as a person, though he hadn't verbalized this to his coach yet, and he really couldn't understand why these press persecutions were occurring.

Expectations were running rampant that the Longhorns would not only win the Southwest Conference in '75, but that they also had the ingredients necessary to win another National Championship. As they prepared for their opening game against Colorado State at Memorial Stadium, the Longhorns were already ranked twelfth in the country, based in large part on the strength of the UT returning lettermen, and, not surprisingly, because of a sophomore sensation by the name of Earl Campbell. As Earl had anticipated, his name appeared on the depth chart for the home opener.

Roosevelt Leaks, Earl's friend and mentor, had graduated the previous year, and was the top draft pick of the Baltimore Colts. Leaks had finished third in the balloting for the Heisman Trophy, an award Earl began to hear more and more about. Still living something of a sheltered life, however, he didn't quite understand the significance of this trophy, which was given to the best college football player in the nation.

Earl started the season against Colorado State with a bang, rushing for 103 yards on 13 attempts and scoring a touchdown, for a final score of 46-0. This convincing win encouraged many Texas supporters in their belief that a conference title and national championship were inevitable.

In contrast to his freshman year, Earl's second college year found him with something different to do after home games. Though he still headed to Jester Hall with Reuna, this year he also had his twin brothers, Tim and Steve, in Austin with him to hang out and cut up with after Reuna left. Ken Dabbs had scored another recruiting *coup* for the Longhorns by securing permission from Ann Campbell to take her "terrible two" down to Austin on football scholarships.

Like Earl, both boys were big in size and were gifted on the football field. Tim would see a great deal of playing time at defensive end during his freshman year. Steve, however, had to battle a knee injury. The important thing to Earl was that they were there with him to ease the loneliness that continued to creep inside him after the fans and Reuna had all gone home. The twins' arrival meant that Earl now had family close by, and he could watch over them so that "Momma wouldn't have to worry about them, 'cause they were a little on the wild side, you know!"

With their solid showing in the first game, the Longhorns moved up to eighth in the national polls. Next, they traveled to the University of Washington for their second meeting with the Huskies in as many years. The game results were much the same as the previous year. Texas found themselves on the winning end, 28-10. This time, Earl had a *huge* game. He rushed for 128 yards on 27 attempts, and scored three touchdowns in the process. This was Earl's finest showing to date for the Longhorns, and his average of 150 yards over two games had him well on track for the goal he had silently vowed to achieve at the beginning of the year.

After this game, Earl did something totally out of the ordinary: *he talked to the media.* He told the reporters, "I've always felt that the best running backs are flat-footed and bow-legged, so I guess that makes me O.K. at what I do!" It wasn't much to go on, but it was becoming obvious that Earl was finally breaking through the silent shell that he had surrounded himself with during his freshman season.

The third game, against the Red Raiders of Texas Tech, would hold a two-fold significance for the Longhorns. First, it marked the season's initial game against a Southwest Conference opponent. In addition, the Longhorns had to settle a team and school vendetta against one of the two teams that had kept UT from winning the conference the previous year. The game would be played at Memorial Stadium and, more importantly, Earl Campbell would be starting at running back. The end result was a 42-18 pounding of the Red Raiders. The Longhorns' sophomore running back scorched the defense for 150 yards on 18 carries and scored two touchdowns. Thus far, Earl was still exceeding his personal goal by averaging an incredible 150 yards in each of the first three games.

The Longhorns' solid play, fueled by the running abilities of Earl Campbell, had now raised UT to a number-seven ranking. The result of their pride and determination in maintaining this ranking was a 61-7 pounding of Utah State the following week. Since the 'Horns were obviously the superior team from the opening kickoff, Earl was used sparingly. He carried the ball only five times for 57 yards, and scored just one touchdown. Earl's lack of playing time in the game kept him from achieving his per-game goal, which only served to double his commitment to make up for lost time at the next game.

The time arrived for the Longhorns' annual Cotton Bowl showdown with the Sooners of Oklahoma. The Selmon brothers were still the foundation of the Sooner program's strength. As always, the game was a nationally televised event, held in the circus-like atmosphere of Dallas and the State Fair week. As in the previous year, Oklahoma was ranked second in the nation and Texas held the number five seed.

The game was another emotional, hard-fought battle. Many members of the Oklahoma team instituted the fine art of "trash talking" for the game as another method of intimidation, but Earl never let the bad-mouthing bother him. He chose instead to let his style of play do the talking. Unfortunately for Coach Royal, Earl, and the rest of the Longhorn team, their determined effort wasn't enough. The Longhorns fell to the powerful Sooner team with a score of 24-17. Earl managed 95 yards on 12 carries, but his efforts fell far short of his self-established goal. The Selmon brothers also managed to keep him out of the end zone.

Although Earl's best wasn't good enough in this game, his play prompted Barry Switzer to announce to a national media audience, "Earl Campbell is the only football player I know who could have gone directly from high school to the NFL and [could have] *made* it!" Once again, a knowledgeable opponent offered strong words of praise.

The Oklahoma loss hurt Earl even more deeply than had previous losses, because he once again witnessed how belligerent the media could be. Coach Royal personally took the media heat for the team's loss.

Earl remembers, "They could be your best friend or your worst enemy. It all depended how you played — this week, *not* in the past."

Unfortunate as the loss may have been, this second consecutive beating by Oklahoma marked the beginning of a close friendship between Earl and Coach Royal. Because of the intense press scrutiny directed at Coach Royal after the Oklahoma game, Earl decided to pay a house call to the coach and his wife, Edith. At first, Royal was curious about why Earl felt he needed to report and show his support. Over time, however, the visits continued on a regular basis, win or lose.

Earl would say, "Just stopped by to say hello, Coach." There was no brown-nosing in his visits, no hidden agendas. Earl just wanted his coach to know that "he'd be there for him if his ox was ever in a ditch."

Understandably confused and perhaps a bit leery at first, the coach soon began to look forward to the visits, even though Earl would usually lie down on the floor with a pillow and fall fast asleep. Upon awakening, Earl would shake the cobwebs from his head before saying, "See y'all later, Coach, Mrs. Royal. Y'all take care now!" Then, just as easily as he'd entered the house, Earl was gone. To this day, Darrell Royal looks back on those visits and recognizes in them Earl's need for a family connection in Austin. He also appreciated Earl's depth of concern for the coach's feelings. The beginning of a rock-solid friendship was formed that season, and it was a friendship that would continue far beyond Earl's college career.

Coach Royal's relationship with, and increasing respect for, Ann Campbell flourished as well during this period. Ann would often write to tell him about the prayers that were being said for him, his family, and the Longhorn team. Royal appreciated the concern and encouragement these letters showed, and he decided to stop by Ann's house in Tyler for a visit while returning to Austin from a recruiting trip. As it turned out, Coach Royal caught her off guard because his visit was unannounced. The house was immaculate nonetheless. Although short, the visit was pleasant, and went a long way in solidifying the friendship between these two wise people.

Finally the time came for Coach Royal to leave. As he walked out towards his car, Ann called to him, "Coach Royal, when you originally came to recruit my Earl, did you ever think it'd turn out to where we'd be this good of friends?"

Not being one to offer a quick response, especially to such a personal question, Royal thought for a few moments before responding, "I thought we could, if we'd both give it a chance. After all, we both have Earl's best interests at heart."

After hearing this, Ann simply turned toward the door and said, "All right," before entering the house.

As he got to know Ann better, Royal came to understand that Earl's visits to his own home in Austin were made out of respect. Ann Campbell had raised her children right, teaching them to respect their elders and listen to them.

Coach Royal had become quite fond of Earl's big, loud, happy, loving family. He was impressed with how close-knit they were, and could well understand how Earl felt lost without his family's daily support. Royal remembered his own loneliness as a child, and recognized Earl's need for a father figure.

The Longhorns were scheduled next to meet the Arkansas Razorbacks, this year in Fayetteville. The game was to be broadcast nationally and was of major importance because it was an intra-conference game. Beyond that, each team had its own fierce agenda. Texas had dropped from fifth to eighth in the polls after the OU game, while Arkansas wanted to avenge their previous year's embarrassment and make a big leap up from their number-twenty poll position. The Razorbacks were out to get Earl in particular, because in the previous year he had broken a close game wide open just four minutes before the half. Arkansas was mentally and physically prepared to defeat UT and Earl Campbell.

The game was a dogfight from the opening kickoff to the final gun, but the Razorbacks still couldn't find the proper combinations to control Earl. He rushed 20 times for 83 yards and one touchdown, in a 24-18 UT triumph. This was a well-deserved victory in a very difficult place to play. The win over the Razorbacks kept the 'Horns undefeated in their conference. They were gaining on their quest for yet another championship and invitation to the Cotton Bowl. As could be expected, the return trip to Austin was joyous, as members of the Longhorn team began to understand and appreciate the true gem they had in Earl Campbell.

The remainder of the Longhorns' schedule was to be played against their always formidable Southwest Conference foes, beginning with the Rice Owls at Memorial Stadium. Although Rice players and students are well-known for their academic achievements, their football skills had always come up short when compared to the much larger universities. Nonetheless, they always played with heart, regardless of the final score. This game would be no different, as the feisty Owls were outmuscled, and fell 41-9 in a valiant effort. Earl had a mediocre day with only 58 yards on nine carries. Most impressive for the Rice Owls was that they managed to keep him from tasting pay dirt.

Maintaining a seed of eighth in the polls, the 'Horns next traveled to Dallas to face the Southern Methodist Mustangs. SMU always played against Texas with a fervor, and the Ponies firmly believed this was *their* year, especially since they were performing in front of their home crowd. To SMU's credit, they played an extremely physical game, but they were no match for the running abilities of Earl Campbell, who broke their hearts on that November afternoon. Texas came away victorious, 30-22, and Earl finished with awe-inspiring statistics: 160 yards rushing on 28 carries, with two touchdowns. To be sure, Earl Campbell was becoming a household sports name, not only in Texas, but around the entire country. Young aspiring players everywhere began to emulate his "run 'em over" style of play.

Moving up to number seven, Texas set their sights on the Baylor Bears, one of the teams who had embarrassed them the previous year. This year's game was to be played at UT's Memorial Stadium, a hostile environment even for the toughest of opponents. This game would signify another of Coach Royal's proudest moments for Earl. Royal played Earl on two separate occasions as a down lineman for the 'Horns' goal line defense. Both times, the Longhorns stopped Baylor in their tracks, furthering Coach Royal's belief that Earl could accomplish anything that was asked of him.

Truth be told, Earl enjoyed those rare moments when he got to grind it out with the linemen. He liked to prove to the opposition the incredible amount of strength he held in his massive frame. The game was much closer than the final score, 37-21, but the Longhorns were once again victorious. Earl rushed for 123 yards on 31 carries, with two touchdowns. This was the first time Coach Royal had called Earl's number over thirty times. It can only be assumed that the Bears were smarting on their return trip to Waco, with visions of Earl Campbell on both sides of the ball firmly embedded in their minds as well as their aching bodies.

Still maintaining their number seven ranking, the 'Horns easily manhandled the Texas Christian Horned Frogs, 27-11, at Memorial Stadium. It was their last home game of the year, and Earl didn't let the crowd down. He scored a touchdown on 41 yards gained. It was his lowest output of the season because Coach Royal called his number a mere nine times. The coach had decided to rest Earl for what was sure to be a Southwest Conference showdown. The following week they would be facing a Texas A&M team that was ranked second in the nation and was desperate for revenge.

If Earl had been confused by the unique traditions the Aggie team and supporters brought with them to Memorial Stadium the previous year, then he was thoroughly boggled on his first trip to College Station. As A&M was long known for its military foundation, Earl found himself surrounded during warm-ups by cadets, with sabers drawn to keep any unwanted or unnecessary individuals off the field of battle. To the Aggies, a football field is just that, a battlefield. As such, only those involved in the war should be granted access to the field.

Another tradition that thoroughly baffled the neophyte visitor was that the Aggie student body and alumni population stood for the entire game, never sitting down, not even during time-outs or at halftime.

Most young men coming into this atmosphere for the first time would be intimidated, but not Earl. In fact, he was complimentary of the show of support that followers gave the Aggie team. He began to understand how these two schools became involved in this bitterest of rivalries. Unlike most of his contemporaries, Earl never displayed animosity toward any individual or team he was playing against. His main concern was winning for the team on which he was playing.

The Tyler Rose: The Earl Campbell Story

In what proved to be a brutally physical game, The Longhorns were no match for the offensive and defensive strength of the Aggies. The latter's defense swarmed after the ball and held Earl to a scant 40 yards on 15 carries, with no touchdowns scored. This containment of Earl Campbell was a major feat for the Aggies.

Unfortunately, the defeat at the hands of the Aggies would have much deeper ramifications than simply being a humbling experience. The game placed the Longhorns in a three-way tie with Arkansas and Texas A&M for the Southwest Conference championship. The tiebreaker decision was that the school who had most recently been to a Cotton Bowl would be forced to waive its position. Thus it was that Arkansas, with its only Southwest Conference defeat having come at the hands of Texas, found itself with a Cotton Bowl invitation by process of elimination.

The loss to A&M and the consequent elimination from the Cotton Bowl once again rankled the sports media. Articles began to appear, criticizing Coach Royal's decision-making capabilities. Commentators wondered in print and on the air whether he had "lost his touch" with his players. They began to question his age and years of service, never once mentioning Royal's accomplishments over the past nineteen years. Even the players were quizzed about their thoughts on whether or not their coach had "lost his fastball."

This infuriated Earl, and he steadfastly defended his coach. "I don't pay any attention to what y'all are saying, 'cause I was always taught by my parents to respect my elders, and I'm gonna do just that. My job is to do what I'm told and play football. That's the least I can do for Coach Royal, since he's the one responsible for me being where I'm at today. That's all I have to say, thank you!"

Earl was starting to feel his oats with the media. He was always careful not to do or say anything that would incite negative comments about himself, his team, or his coach. He didn't believe that the media's treatment of Coach Royal was at all ethical, and he certainly didn't wish to become part of their feeding frenzy.

The '75 Longhorn team accepted an invitation to play in the Bluebonnet Bowl, held in the Houston Astrodome. Although they had slipped from fifth to ninth in the rankings, the 'Horns were facing a very intense, tenth-ranked Colorado Buffalo team.

Texas ultimately defeated their worthy opponents from Colorado, 38-21. Until halftime, however, the Buffaloes manhandled the 'Horns — definitely an embarrassment since the game was being played in the state of Texas. In the locker room at half-time, no one could exactly place a finger on the team's mood, but each player took close inventory of themselves and the less than acceptable game they were playing. Each of them realized that a blowout at the hands of Colorado would mean another round of unmerciful tirades against their coach, the man who had taken a keen interest in their recruiting, football, schooling, and personal lives.

Above and beyond the inventory they each took, they also found something that had been lost since the final gun went off at the A&M game: *pride*. Their newly rediscovered pride fueled them to play with such intensity during the second half that after the final gun went off, something significant occurred. Earl Campbell, sophomore, was voted the Bluebonnet Bowl Offensive Player of the Game. His brother, Tim, only a freshman, was voted Defensive Player of the Game for his fierce play at defensive end. Having only three years of college experience between them, both of these young men proved to an entire viewing nation the remarkable talents that God had bestowed upon the Campbell family.

As in his freshman season, Earl achieved All Southwest Conference. He was also voted All American at The University of Texas. These votes were cast by coaches nationwide in acknowledgment of the awesome skills which the young man possessed. Earl also attained his goal of a thousand yards rushing, scoring a total of thirteen touchdowns in the process.

At the end of the spring semester, however, Coach Royal was forced to put a damper on Earl's accomplishments. Royal was a stickler for the rule that his players perform in the classroom as well as on the field. Despite his good intentions in the beginning, Earl had failed English during the spring semester. Even though his other grades were good, and his total GPA was acceptable, Coach Royal's principles would not allow him to ignore the failing grade. He felt obligated to stick by his rules, regardless of who the student was.

Reluctantly he sent Earl back to Tyler that summer. Earl was put to work at Brookshire Brothers grocery store, loading trucks during the height of the Texas summer heat. This was much more than a punishment. Royal used the opportunity to force Earl to think about what his priorities truly were, and to teach the young man a lesson he'd never forget. Above and beyond the humiliation, Earl did do a lot of thinking, and reconfirmed his commitment to never return to the life he had left behind in Tyler. His resolve was reinforced each time he lifted one of the many heavy items onto the waiting trucks in the sweltering Texas heat. Though his methods were admittedly harsh, Coach Royal achieved what he set out to do. After that summer, Earl never failed another class.

Expectations were running at a fever pitch during the 1976 summer camp, as the coaches and players once again believed that this would definitely be their year for a conference and national championship. Virtually all the starters returned from the previous year, led by senior superstar, Raymond Clayborn. A confirmed spokesperson for the team, Raymond was born with the gift of gab, and was able to converse on any level, about anything, to anyone who would listen.

Raymond's challenge was to lead a team that was still smarting from the previous season-ending loss to arch rival, Texas A&M. They were also determined to deflect the heat Coach Royal had been taking because of their playing, not his coaching. The team was on a definite mission to prove the media wrong, and each person on the team vowed to accomplish this mission through their efforts, not through idle words to an unfriendly media.

In an amazing string of unexpected calamities, fate would deal Coach Royal the worst luck he had encountered in his twenty years of coaching. It began during summer workouts. As the offense was practicing various non-contact running plays, Earl took a pitchout and cut outside, then headed north-south up the field. As he made the cut, Earl felt something snap in the back of his upper leg, a strange and painful feeling which he had never before experienced. After the initial snap, an unbearable pain literally sent him to the turf in agony. No one had hit him, nor had he hurdled anyone. Rather, a slight misstep had left him with a torn hamstring.

Unfortunately, the remedy for a badly torn hamstring involves much more than a few days' rest and relaxation. The hamstring is analogous to a rubber band in the back of the leg, and once it is stretched beyond proportion, the result is a long and painful healing process. For Earl, whose current and future livelihood revolved around playing football, the injury also became a mental handicap. Earl's personal beliefs dictated that he must never let his teammates or Coach Royal down, no matter how bad the odds appeared to be, but with the torn hamstring, he found himself at the mercy of his own body. This was something he simply wasn't prepared to deal with.

As if Earl's injury weren't catastrophic enough, many other key players received devastating injuries. Coach Royal was forced to insert freshmen and sophomores into a lineup where skilled veterans were supposed to be. The situation grew increasingly dismal as many of the intended starters found themselves preparing on a day-to-day basis for the season opener against Boston College. With great disappointment, Earl finally accepted that there was virtually nothing that could be done to expedite the healing of his badly torn hamstring. The only treatments available to him were whirlpools, massages, and rest. The ultimate test would be in Earl's ability to recuperate without compounding the injury in the process.

Earl's frequent visits to Coach Royal's house gave the coach occasion to introduce him to many of the Royal family's friends. For example, there were Ernest and Joyce Owens, who had first become acquainted with Royal during his early years of coaching. Quiet and unassuming, the Owens had worked towards building a land development dynasty in the Dallas-Fort Worth area. Through their friend Darrell Royal, they had also become avid fans of Texas Longhorn football. Royal introduced them to Earl Campbell and, over a period of time, they became good friends with the quiet superstar.

Ernest and Joyce had a customized Trailways bus, complete with easy chairs, televisions, and refrigerators, which they would drive to the Longhorn home games and park adjacent to the stadium. The bus was easy to spot and was a comfortable place to relax before and after games.

The Owens extended an open invitation to Earl to use their bus whenever they were in town. This allowed Earl a place to get away from the screaming fans and the media, who were constantly deluging him with requests for autographs or interviews.

Royal and the Owens also introduced Earl to various country musicians, whom he got to know on a personal level. Long an admirer of country music, Earl found that it helped him wind down after the games. Earl and Reuna would sit in that bus in the oversized easy chairs, listening to the artists who took turns showcasing their talents. Little did Earl know that these same musicians were equally appreciative for the show that he had recently given them on the football field.

It was on the Owens' bus that Coach Royal experienced his most gratifying remembrance of Earl Campbell, and it was one that had nothing to do with running a football. It would take place after the last game of that year.

Although many of their starters were out with injuries, the Long-horns were still ranked seventh as they headed into their opening game against Boston College. Earl was determined to play and was suited up, though he was fully aware that he couldn't "cut" east or west on the field. The opposing team realized that Campbell could only rush one way with the ball — straight ahead. This type of play was a high-risk gamble for both Earl and Coach Royal, because the hamstring could only get worse in a full contact situation. Both coach and player knew that there was little or no "stretch" to the rubber band inside the back of Earl's enormous leg.

The game turned out to be an omen of things to come for the '76 Longhorns, as UT went down in defeat at the hands of an unranked opponent, 14-13. A merciless Boston team caught them totally off guard. Earl managed only 23 yards on five carries. Several of the Boston College defensive players taunted him about his inepti-tude when running with the ball. More than anything else, this taunting weighed heaviest on Earl because he realized that had he been healthy, the outcome of the game would have been totally different. Thus he began the season in a spirit of frustration.

As usual, the media were unrelenting on the coach who was desperately trying to perform a magician's act while juggling his available troops. In a way, Coach Royal's legendary status was working against him now. Throughout his years of triumph, reporters and fans alike had also come to subscribe to his theory that losing was not an option. Defeat at the hands of lowly Boston College created a furor among the "Royal bashers." No sympathy was given to the coach, no consideration for what he was up against with his injury-riddled troops.

Fortunately for the Longhorns, their next game was against North Texas State, a small college that was not a member of the

The Tyler Rose: The Earl Campbell Story

Southwest Conference. Even though the Longhorns had dropped twelve points in the polls, to nineteenth, they were still considered a huge favorite in the game, scheduled for play at Memorial Stadium. Earl suited up once again, but hoped the team would enjoy a first half blowout, so that he could give some much-needed rest to his painful hamstring injury.

It was not to be. Earl was forced to play the entire game by sheer determination. He amassed 208 yards on 32 carries and scored one touchdown. What was even worse than Earl having to play the entire contest was the final score, 17-14. The powerful Texas Long-horns had just barely defeated a team that, on paper, didn't qualify to be on the same playing field. And after the game, Earl was in such pain that he couldn't even stop by the Owens' bus. He immediately bid good-bye to Reuna and headed for the training room.

The last thing Earl had expected that day was having to play the entire game against a team that wasn't even in the same division. At that moment, he realized the team, and Coach Royal, were in deep trouble.

For the first time in many years, the Texas Longhorn football team found themselves unranked as they prepared for their Southwest Conference opener against Rice at Rice Stadium. Still, although neither team was ranked, Texas was clearly a huge favorite, based on their humiliation of the Owls in years past. Despite their many recent challenges, pride and determination overshadowed all else, and the 'Horns manhandled the Owls, 42-15. Texas was reinstated to sixteenth place in the eyes of the national pollsters. Still playing on the badly torn hamstring, Earl pounded out 78 yards on 18 carries.

After the game, Earl had to undergo what was becoming a ritual massage, whirlpool, and ice treatment before he could return to Austin. Remembering that season, he recalls that this was the worst he had ever felt in his life, even though he was playing the game that he loved so dearly.

Hook 'Em 'Horns

Coach Royal had no time to ponder the past as his team prepared for their annual trip to the Cotton Bowl. They would be facing a very determined and powerful Oklahoma team, currently ranked third in the nation. Gone from the Sooner program were the Selmon brothers, drafted by various professional teams. They were replaced by an even hungrier group of individuals whose brash talk and cocky style of play made them perfect for the strategy that Coach Barry Switzer intended to use against the injury riddled Longhorns.

Despite his injuries, Earl was fully prepared for this yearly battle. He had learned that this game was played for pride between two states and two illustrious football powers, and he was determined to do his part. Reuna drove to Dallas for the game. As in the past, this game was once again to be broadcast by ABC Television to a nation of zealous football addicts. Earl was certain that not only his mother but the entire city of Tyler would be in front of their TV sets, following each play.

In one of the most grueling, hand-wringing games of his career, Darrell Royal watched his valiant warriors battle the powerful Sooner team to a 6-6 tie. Earl endured a punishing game. He carried the ball for 99 yards on 27 attempts before Coach Royal finally pulled him out of the game. Earl was devastated, feeling in his heart that he had let down his coach, his team, and The University of Texas. Tears streamed down his face as he limped off the field, fully believing that his peers felt that he hadn't given his usual 110%.

Coach Royal saw the anguish on Earl's face and said to his student and friend, "Son, you did just fine with what you were able to do. You can't let it get you down!"

Earl would have liked to believe that, but couldn't. Instead, he saw his season, and possibly his career, slipping away. He felt that with the increasingly poor results he was producing, any and all chances of achieving his ultimate goal of playing in the National

Football League were being washed down the drain. All of this was extraordinarily distressing to Earl. He had been betrayed by his once-powerful body — something he'd believed could never happen.

When the gun finally went off to signal the end of the game, a national television audience focused on a picture of Coach Darrell Royal, bent over with his hands resting on both knees, staring aimlessly at the ground. Frustration and dejection were written on his face, for he knew that his troops had done an exemplary job, yet they were sure to be criticized by the unforgiving media for not winning the game. Despite the fact that they were playing shorthanded, and Earl had to be taken from the game, nothing short of winning would suffice for the staunch supporters and followers of Texas Longhorn football.

One very interested party witnessing Coach Royal's dejection was Ann Campbell, who had watched the entire game at home, with all the other family members gathered around. Ann was shocked by Coach Royal's reaction after the game and decided to sit down to write her coach and friend a letter.

In a most sincere message, Ann admonished Darrell Royal because, as she wrote, her coach "had put his head down for everyone to see." She felt that as a leader of men, especially her boys, he should never show visible signs of dejection toward the outcome of their performance. She finished the letter by stating, "I'd like to recommend you to a Man who sits high, yet looks low."

After receiving the letter, Coach Royal was moved by its sincerity and the truth of its message. In fact, the letter had such an impact on him that he kept it. To this day he'll pull it out on occasion as a reminder — not only of the powerful yet simple message it contains, but of the remarkably humble and incredibly wise woman who has won the respect of so many people.

Although the game against the Sooners ended in a tie, it was played well enough in the eyes of the pollsters to drop the Longhorns three points in the rankings to thirteenth. They next faced Southern Methodist, an unranked team who hadn't beaten the 'Horns in their past nine encounters. Texas emerged victorious, 13-12, but was dropped to fifteenth place nonetheless, because the pollsters considered the game a poor showing. Earl had suited up and given his all, but the pain had taken a heavy toll. He had rushed for a mere 57 yards on 17 carries.

So far Earl had scored only one touchdown this season, and *that* was against lowly North Texas State. His performance each week continued to have an adverse affect on his mental well-being. Neither Reuna, Tim, nor Steve knew what to say to console him as he headed for his mandatory post-game training room ritual.

It seemed to Earl that neither the media nor the fans cared anything about what it means to play in pain. To Earl, it meant having to immediately forget his poor performance against SMU and, despite his physical and emotional agony, concentrate on the sixth-ranked, finely-tuned Texas Tech Red Raiders, who were next on the Longhorns' schedule. Tech was stacked full of veteran players, obsessed by the desire to make amends for their embarrassment the previous year at Memorial Stadium. And when the final gun sounded, they had made these amends in a hard fought, bruising game in which the Red Raiders emerged victorious, 31-28. Earl was used only sparingly, but he gained 65 yards on seven carries.

More importantly, Coach Royal decided that continuing to play Earl meant the distinct possibility of permanent damage for his star player, as it was obvious that Earl's physical problem was getting worse, not better. Because of Coach Royal's decision, Earl was taken out in the second quarter and benched. For such a proud young man, this was the ultimate humiliation, but Earl was forced to accept this benching over the course of the next four games.

The twentieth-ranked Longhorns next played host to the nineteenth-ranked University of Houston Cougars, and were caught off guard by the powerful Cougar team, 30-0. Earl agonized as he watched his team struggle, for he realized that each defeat meant another nail in Coach Royal's coffin at the hands of an unrelenting media. The Houston defeat also signaled the end of the longest unbeaten home record in Memorial Stadium history. The UT winning record of 42 games at home dated back to October 5, 1968. Worse, once again the 'Horns were unranked by the pollsters, and diehard Longhorn supporters were getting very nervous.

The Longhorns dug deeply into their supply of pride to come away with a solid trouncing of the TCU Horned Frogs, 34-7. Although they won handily, UT was still not ranked among the top 25 teams in the nation. A feeling of futility permeated the air in the Longhorn locker room.

Playing on the road in Waco against the Bears of Baylor University, Coach Royal's boys were no match for the clearly superior green and gold. The final score, 20-10, didn't fully disclose the beating suffered by the 'Horns at the hands of this Southwest Conference foe. Earl was still relegated to the bench. He was only too painfully aware of what was in store the following week when the eleventh ranked Texas A&M Aggies would pay a visit for their annual Thanksgiving Day game, which was, of course, scheduled for national television broadcast.

Pride can only carry a team so far if they are outmatched and outmuscled. In a game totally dominated by the Aggies from kickoff until the final gun, an overflow Memorial Stadium crowd witnessed a convincing 27-3 Longhorn defeat at the hands of their bitter rivals. After watching this debacle from the bench, Earl had seen enough. Injury or no injury, he informed Coach Royal that he wished to play in the Longhorns' final game of the season against Arkansas.

Royal had extreme reservations about Earl's request to play. He was aware that further damage to the hamstring injury could be devastating to the remainder of the young man's college and professional career. Earl, however, was unyielding. He literally begged Coach Royal to allow him to finish the season on the field with the rest of his battered and beaten teammates. He felt he had to prove to his team, his coach and his fans that he *was* willing to go the extra mile, regardless of the pain he felt or the consequences he faced.

Just the sight of Earl suited up gave his teammates an undeniable boost of pride and determination. They knew that he was jeopardizing the remainder of his career to ensure they went out on a winning note. And winning is exactly what they did, handing the Razorbacks a punishing 29-12 defeat. During the three-and-a-half hours it took to play the game, Earl forgot about the pain and became a man possessed. He carried the ball 32 times for 131 yards, scoring two touchdowns in the process. But it was a bittersweet victory for the Longhorns, for they finished the season 5-5-1, placing fifth in the Southwest Conference. This had been their worst season since 1956, the year before Darrell Royal had become head coach.

In the locker room after the game, a teammate told Earl to head for the media room, where Coach Royal was about to begin an unscheduled press conference. As he entered the large room, Earl could see the reporters gathered around the coach. Everyone clearly seemed concerned about more than the results of the game. Because the room was packed with cameras and microphones, Earl had to stand on a folding chair at the very back of the room to see and hear. He was dressed only in sweat socks, football pants, and a cutoff T-shirt.

Earl didn't quite grasp what was happening as the legendary coach prepared to speak. Briefly looking up from the mass of microphones assembled in front of him, Darrell Royal made eye contact with his young protégé before reading from his prepared statement. It was at the moment their eyes locked that Earl finally understood what his coach was doing. He was calling it quits.

Royal began by addressing the "changing times" in the sport of football. He said he understood that many schools were looking for more youthful coaches who could better relate to the new breed of recruits. He addressed the issue of Title IX, which was altering the face of the game by forcing schools to establish a degree of parity between men and women in all sports. Finally, Coach Royal admitted that the hardest part about stepping down from his prestigious position was leaving his coaches and players, all of whom he had painstakingly handpicked. Although it appeared that he was leaving on a down note, Darrell Royal felt just the opposite. He firmly believed that he was leaving on a positive note because of the many outstanding football players developing in the UT program.

The most difficult part of all, he informed the crowd assembled before him, was that "I'm leaving Earl Campbell, who is most definitely in a league of his own."

And that was it, the end of a dynasty in college football. After that, Coach Royal fielded what seemed like an endless stream of questions from the media. To this day he fondly recalls that Earl Campbell, his good friend, was the only player who remained for the entire retirement announcement, and the question and answer period that followed.

Earl was in shock as he stood on the folding chair, listening to his mentor say goodbye. Tears formed in his eyes; he felt betrayed. He had entered UT assuming that Coach Royal had made a deal with him. The deal had begun three years earlier on a signature of intent, and Earl just assumed it meant that as long as he played for UT, he would play for Darrell Royal. Now the old familiar feelings were coming back, uncomfortably similar to those he'd had seven years earlier when Butch La Croix exited from his life. They were feelings of emptiness, guilt, and loneliness, and they were most disturbing.

As he went back to his locker, Earl thought about all of the other reasons for his coach's retirement, those having nothing to do with what Royal had outlined at the press conference. The media were certainly instrumental; Earl was painfully aware that the myriad of cutting remarks on paper and on the air were responsible for turning a three-time national championship coach from a hero into a scapegoat.

But the real reason for his coach stepping down, he knew, was the refusal of the governing powers of college football to put an end to the underhanded dealings taking place at many top schools. Though Coach Royal had proven to them that cheating was standard procedure by many schools, to date they had still taken no corrective action. Earl was well aware that Coach Royal had feared losing even *him* to another university, because of the "bonuses" that were being offered. This, of course, was why the coach had been so relieved when Earl informed him that he couldn't be bought.

Coach Royal had long since come to know that cheating of any sort just wasn't in Earl's repertoire. Earl, in turn, took pride in the fact that The University of Texas was never involved in any investigations during Darrell Royal's tenure. Above all else, integrity was what counted most to Earl.

That night, after he finished showering, Earl left the locker room, knowing that Reuna had left for Tyler hours ago. The sense of betrayal he'd originally felt had subsided, and Earl began to think about the brilliant man Darrell Royal truly was. Not only was he a successful teacher and coach, but Royal was also an excellent politician in an institution where politics are an integral part of the job. Coach Royal had successfully politicked for twenty years before finally calling it quits. He had made his mark in football history and was leaving as the game was about to change, sadly, for the worse.

As Earl left the stadium, he witnessed something he'd never seen before. Two men, obviously friends, were departing for separate destinations. As they were saying their final good-byes, both men embraced and verbally expressed their love for one another.

The Tyler Rose: The Earl Campbell Story

"They weren't gay or anything," Earl recalls. "They were just good friends who were expressing their true feelings for one another." After observing this, Earl realized it was the first time he had ever seen two males openly express feelings in this way, and he was deeply moved.

Shortly thereafter, he spotted Ernest Owens' bus outside the main gate, engine running and noise filtering out from the large windows. He decided to visit his friends, knowing full well that Coach Royal was probably inside. As the doors opened, Earl spotted Darrell Royal in the rear of the bus, sitting with Jimmy Dean, the famous country singer who retired to become well-known in the sausage and bacon industry. As Royal saw Earl approaching, he stood up, wondering just what to say that might help alleviate the pain he knew he had inflicted on his friend without warning. Instead, it was Earl who spoke first, after acknowledging Jimmy Dean's presence.

"Coach, I just saw the most amazing thing outside the stadium. Two men who were friends were saying good-bye to each other. Instead of shaking hands, they hugged each other and expressed their love, verbally, and they weren't queer or nothin'. Well, this touched me 'cause I didn't know what I was gonna say to you tonight, in the event I saw you. Anyway, I just want you to know that no matter what happens, I'll always love you."

And that was that. Earl hugged Darrell Royal, Royal reciprocated . . . and Jimmy Dean just sat there with tears in his eyes, wishing that all those people who'd ever believed Darrell Royal to be a racist could see what was happening at that moment.

Darrell Royal states without hesitation that Earl Campbell's finest quality is that, "He's a loyal, caring friend. When Earl Campbell takes someone as a friend, there's nothing he wouldn't do for them."

Hook 'Em 'Horns

The '76 football year proved to be a most difficult time in Earl Campbell's life. Enduring the pain from his hamstring injury left him doubting his own potential and, for a brief period of time, he even thought about quitting the one sure thing that had brought him success. He felt certain that professional teams had written him off as a potential draft choice. And the retirement of Coach Royal had cast yet another shadow over the plans he had envisioned for the future.

The only truly bright spot that year was in his schooling. Earl passed all his courses, which kept him on schedule for a degree in Speech Communications. With the probability of a degree in sight, Earl knew he could count on some kind of career outside of football. After much soul-searching, however, Earl realized that he couldn't just quit on himself or his fellow teammates. He wouldn't let down the friends with whom he had practiced and played for three rigorous seasons.

He reasoned that, "We had come this far together, so I might as well see it through and let the chips fall where they may." Little could Earl have known that the best years of his life still lay ahead, and, if he stayed focused, he would soar to heights he had only dreamed of.

As preparations for the 1977 season began, there was a widely felt, yet unspoken, optimism in the locker room. This season would showcase the pinnacle of Darrell Royal's recruiting program, with players such as Earl Campbell, Brad Shearer, Alfred Jackson, George James, Morgan Copeland, and Rick Ingraham being asked to stand and deliver.

If the team's optimism was subdued, it was, in large part, because of the one unknown factor in the equation: their new and largely untested coach. Everyone had become adjusted to Coach Royal and his expectations, but no one was aware of what their newly elected leader, Fred Akers, was capable of doing. True, he'd been the backfield coach at Texas during Earl's freshman year, working under the direct supervision of Coach Royal. But then Akers had left after that season to become head coach at Wyoming, seemingly worlds apart from the Texas campus and its illustrious football program. Unknown to almost everyone on the Longhorn staff, however, Akers entered into his contract with Wyoming with a stipulation attached. If either the University of Arkansas or University of Texas had a head coaching position available, he would be free to pursue this opening.

To say the least, Akers was shocked by the retirement of his one-time boss as a result of the mediocre showing by the Longhorns during the '76 season. But, of course, when he was offered the position, Fred Akers gladly accepted, aware of the talented players he would be inheriting. This was the opportunity of a lifetime for Akers, who considered himself blessed that in his first year as head coach of the Longhorns he would benefit from Darrell Royal's dream team of recruiting classes. He planned to make the most of it.

Coach Akers is a no-nonsense man, especially when it comes to football and his players. His first order of business was to meet with each of his players to inform them of exactly what he expected from them, individually and as part of the team. He met with Earl on a day when both of them were dressed up in suits and ties, after having had their picture taken together for the front cover of the Longhorn media guide. After the picture session, Akers asked Earl to step into his office for their one-on-one conversation. As was his nature, Coach Akers got right to the point with his premier running back.

"I need to know, Mr. Campbell. Do you want to run the ball for this university?"

Earl was taken off guard by the question, since he believed everyone knew that his sole purpose for living was to run the football for the Longhorns.

"Yes sir, I do — real bad," was Earl's simple response.

"Well then, we're going to see how bad you want it. My plan

is to make you the focal point of our offense, giving you the ball between 35 and 40 times a game. We're going to get rid of the wishbone attack and go to a straight back offense with Johnnie (Ham) Jones as your blocking back. You will be the tailback in the 'I' formation. Are you acquainted with the straight back formation, Mr. Campbell?"

Though Earl was in a state of shock, he composed himself long enough to answer the question. As he was familiar with the straight back formation from his years at John Tyler High School, a distinct gleam came to his eyes.

"Yes sir, I believe I can handle that formation," Earl declared confidently.

"Good, Mr. Campbell. You're going to have to prove it to me, and it's going to take an awful lot of hard work on your part. I want you down to 220 pounds by the time the season begins. That's a key ingredient if this is going to work."

Once again, Earl was taken aback, for the season was only six weeks away — and he'd carried 245 pounds on his frame for several consecutive years.

"But coach, I haven't been 220 pounds since my sophomore year in high school. How am I gonna do that in six weeks?" Earl was truly perplexed, and nervous as well, because if he *didn't* get to the desired weight, he knew Coach Akers well enough to know that he would find someone who would.

"Well, Mr. Campbell, I suggest you get with Frank Medina, who will be more than glad to help you devise a strategy!" And that was the end of the conversation. The rest was up to Earl.

Frank Medina was the trainer at Texas. Although barely five feet, two inches tall, he was respected nationally for his knowledge when dealing with athletes. Having previously served as trainer on two different Olympic teams, Medina had chosen to settle in Austin with The University of Texas. Like Fred Akers, Frank Medina was a no-

nonsense man and, when Earl approached him about shedding the pounds, the elderly man simply looked at him and said, "Do you have the desire it's gonna take to do this?"

Realizing this was his last shot at proving himself to the various NFL teams, Earl responded, "Mr. Medina, I'm gonna do whatever it takes to get there."

Medina recognized the sincerity in Earl's eyes and said, "Good. We start tomorrow and everyday thereafter at 6:30 A.M. Don't worry about getting up on time, I'll take care of that!" Earl didn't exactly understand what Medina meant by this last statement, but he would soon find out.

True to his word, Frank Medina dialed Earl Campbell the next morning and, after Earl groggily answered, Medina triumphantly announced in his high-pitched voice, "Earl Campbell, it's 6:30. Time to get up. Meet me downstairs in fifteen minutes." Earl did.

For six consecutive weeks he followed the regimen that the world famous trainer had drawn up. The plan was to shed 25 pounds in 42 days. By 7:00 A.M., Medina and Earl were at the gym, where Earl pounded the heavy bag for an hour while wearing a rubber sweat suit. Next, he went outside to run the track for an hour, still in the sweat suit. Medina stood in the middle of the track, white towel wrapped firmly around his neck.

The early morning summer sun comes up hot in Austin, where the Texas landscape turns from ranch to farm land. That sun glared over Medina's shoulders as he barked orders to Earl on the lawns of the empty practice field. Earl paced himself and stayed focused by marking his path against the passing landscape. As he turned west, he saw the UT tower and imagined it blazing orange for victory. Past the tower, further west, were Lake Austin and Lake Travis. Earl had learned to love the rugged Texas Hill Country with its rock and cedar, so markedly different from his home in Tyler. Thinking about all this as he made his way around the track, he was reminded that he had changed and adjusted once before, and could do it again.

Earl sometimes thought his wily trainer wasn't looking, and he'd slow his pace down, only to hear that loud, squeaky voice scream, "Mr. Campbell, I can't see you, but I *can* hear you, and your footsteps have slowed to a crawl. NOW, PICK UP THE PACE, OR YOU WILL HAVE PROVEN TO ME THAT YOU *DON'T* WANT THIS BAD ENOUGH."

And Earl would do as he was told, not just out of pride but also from the fear that Medina would tell Coach Akers that he was "dogging it." With his new coach, Earl's chief concern was making the cut.

Immediately following the running regimen, it was off to the weight room, where Earl would wear a weighted vest while performing 400 sit-ups. Frank Medina held Earl at the ankles to ensure the exercise was properly done, with no possibility for fudging. And then, as if this weren't enough, Medina would put Earl in the steam room and lock the door. Trouble was, this highly skilled trainer was getting up in years, and often forgot about Earl, leaving him to "cook" well beyond the planned half-hour session. The result was a thoroughly dehydrated young man who would literally drag himself into the shower before heading for a low-fat lunch, served with plenty of liquids to replenish his extremely depleted system. After lunch, Medina released Earl back to Coach Akers and the team. Earl would then put on his pads and practice for the entire afternoon.

All of Earl's teammates were inspired by his commitment to get down to Coach Akers' desired weight. As Rick Ingraham said, "Watching Earl go through that rigorous routine elevated all of us in practice. When we saw how badly Earl wanted it, then all of us adopted the attitude that we would elevate ourselves to his level. Despite all he had been through with Frank Medina, Earl never once slacked off in practice. Watching him out there running over people made all of us want to try harder. We realized this year was our last chance to capture a Southwest Conference Championship."

Earl's desire and determination got him elected team captain that year, along with Brad Shearer, Morgan Copeland, and George James. This honor gave Earl an added inducement to succeed, as the team was looking up to him for leadership and guidance. The good news was that after five-and-a-half weeks of working with Frank Medina, with only a few days to go before the 'Horns' home opener against Boston College, Earl Campbell weighed in at 220 pounds. He could tell that the loss of weight had made him quicker, especially considering he was now going to get a seven-yard head start when running from the tailback position.

One other very significant change came over Earl as a result of his travail: he began to have visions about winning the Heisman Trophy, and even began thinking of the speech he would make when accepting this prestigious award. Before his new training, Earl had dismissed the possibility of the Heisman because of his poor showing and his injury. But the idea was still there, in the back of his mind, and it was mighty appealing. He knew that Tony Dorsett had won the Heisman the previous year, playing tailback for the University of Pittsburgh — and had become an instant millionaire when he was drafted by the Dallas Cowboys. Now Earl was feeling that a similar good fortune was possible for him.

In order for the Heisman to become a reality for Earl, however, several key factors would have to roll in his favor. First and most important, his level of play would have to be exemplary, and this responsibility would rest on his shoulders alone. Secondly, and of nearly equal importance, media reports about both The University of Texas and Earl Campbell would have to be more favorable. Over the past several years, it had become obvious that the media wielded an exorbitant amount of influence over those who voted for the best player in college football. And finally, Earl would need a huge break, somewhere, somehow, along the way. If all these ingredients were in place, he stood a decent chance of being recognized as one of the finalists for the award.

Fred Akers' first game as head coach for the Texas Longhorns was against Boston College, playing before a sellout crowd at Memorial Stadium. This first game proved to be pivotal, as the Texas players were looking to avenge their season opening loss to this same team a year earlier. The 'Horns were also upset because they had entered the season ranked eighteenth in the polls. UT was truly insulted, and felt that the ranking was unfair in light of the fact that the majority of their key players had been injured the previous year. A win for UT would allow Coach Akers the breathing room he needed to prove himself, especially critical to a coach attempting to fill the shoes of a legend.

Coach Akers knew he was blessed with talent, but the ballot was still out on how the team would respond to the new offensive and defensive formations he had installed. Fortunately for him, it wouldn't take long to find out. The Longhorns were unmerciful in their treatment of Boston College, handing them a humiliating 44-0 defeat. Earl got off to a slow start, but finished with 87 yards on 17 carries, scoring one touchdown. Considering the enormous margin of victory, the pollsters immediately moved the 'Horns up to ninth in the national rankings.

With a very kind early season schedule, the Longhorns next found themselves entertaining the Cavaliers of Virginia. This would be the game where Earl finally felt comfortable with his new plays. The Tyler Rose destroyed the Cavalier defense, rushing for 156 yards on 19 carries, and scoring two touchdowns. The final result of the game was as portentous as Earl's statistics, a 68-0 conquest of their ill-fated opponents. The Longhorn team was exuberant, knowing that they were much better than they *or* the press had originally predicted.

In their third game, also played at home, the Longhorns faced

The Tyler Rose: The Earl Campbell Story

Rice in their initial bid to recapture the elusive Southwest Conference crown. Even the wary sportswriters weren't expecting the 72-15 humiliation that Texas slapped on their conference foes. Rice was thoroughly beaten, left to hobble back to Houston to nurse their wounds. Earl had another in what was to become a record-breaking string of phenomenal games. He riddled the Rice defense for 131 yards on only 17 carries, and scored four touchdowns. Considering the combined scores of the first three games — 184-15 — the national media began to pay close attention, especially to those numbers that were being produced by a lighter, faster, and seemingly unstoppable Earl Campbell.

Although the 'Horns were attracting national attention, many Southwest Conference reporters made light of their early successes, since the three teams whom they had beaten so soundly were far from being powerhouses. The papers proclaimed, "A real test for Coach Fred Akers and his Longhorns will be held October 8th when they meet the Sooners of Oklahoma in the Cotton Bowl."

For once, the writers' assessments were accurate. The Texas players and coaches began to prepare, in earnest, for this important contest, each fully aware that they hadn't won in three years. For Earl this game was significant for yet another reason, as it could also provide a major stepping stone in his quest for the Heisman Trophy. If he could play anything like he had against their first three opponents, this game would dramatically elevate his image in the eyes of a nation, especially the Southwest Conference reporters.

As it stood, pre-game hype was extensive, because the number-two team was pitted against the number-five team. There was no denying that neither team held the other in high regard. The rivalry was bitter, the stakes were high, and Earl knew he needed to have not a just a good game, but a *great* one.

The game was a fiercely physical, hard-hitting event, and Fred Akers couldn't possibly have predicted what was to happen in the early stages of the first quarter. On Texas' first offensive series, their starting quarterback, Mark McBath, went down with a broken ankle. Six minutes later, Jon Aune, McBath's replacement, was knocked senseless. This apocalyptic series of misfortunes left the Longhorns with one quarterback, Randy McEachern, who had worked with the practice squad but had never taken a single snap in a regular season game.

Unknown to, but luckily for, Coach Akers and the rest of the Texas squad, McEachern had always paid strict attention during practice, and was more ready than anyone could have anticipated. Just in case, however, Rick Ingraham, the starting offensive guard, issued his own simple orders to the concerned signal caller, "Just give the damn ball to Earl, Randy."

McEachern did just that, following Ingraham's instructions to the letter. He handed the ball to Earl a total of 23 times, who then rushed for 124 yards against the mighty Sooner defense. On one of these running plays, Earl cut right and saw a dead end, then reversed his field and hurdled a Sooner defensive back en route to a 25 yard touchdown scamper. That run, and the subsequent hurdle of the defensive back, was shown on virtually every sportscast in the country, and is widely regarded as the catalyst for the "Heisman Hype" that was to continue with each future game. More importantly, Texas won the ballgame, 13-6, with a novice quarterback and a national television audience in attendance. Indeed, many sports historians have looked back on the '77 Texas/Oklahoma war as the game that officially signaled that Texas had a bona-fide Heisman candidate.

In an interesting reversal of fortune, the Texas Longhorns found themselves replacing the Oklahoma Sooners as the number-two-ranked team in the nation. But their newly acquired celebrity status would be short lived, because the Longhorns had to travel to Fayetteville next to face another powerful team: the Arkansas Razorbacks. Coached by the crafty Lou Holtz, the Razorbacks were proud of their number-eight ranking, and truly felt that no team could beat them in their home stadium. The Razorbacks had prepared well for their foes from the Lone Star State, and felt confident that they could contain the rushing abilities of Earl Campbell. About the only thing they *weren't* prepared for was Earl's pass catching ability. Earl was the man who was affectionately known as "Brickhands" by his teammates.

In a play that will forever be remembered in Texas/Arkansas folklore, young Randy McEachern rolled right, looking to pass, while Earl drifted to the left, all by his lonesome. As McEachern kept rolling, with all his receivers covered, he suddenly spotted Earl on the left sideline, frantically waving his arms.

McEachern later commented, "Earl's eyes were so big, they looked like saucers. All I could think was, 'Please catch it, Earl, *please.'*"

Catch it Earl did, taking off down the left sideline like a bullet shot from a gun. A lone defensive back was standing at the one-yard line, hoping beyond hope that help would arrive, but it didn't. As was his style, Earl chose to run over the defensive back, thoroughly leveling him in the process.

Unfortunately, the referee said Earl's knee had touched at the half-yard line before he had destroyed the smaller defensive back. No matter; on the next play McEachern faked a hand-off to Earl, and the entire Arkansas defense swarmed toward him as Johnnie "Ham" Jones dove into the end zone with the ball.

Despite Arkansas' belief that they could contain Earl, he turned out to be unstoppable. He ran the ball as if possessed by demons. He gained 188 yards on 34 carries, as a nation watched this multi-faceted phenom perform. In the end the Longhorns prevailed, 13-9, this time against a team which was, by any standard, a formidable power. By now, Earl Campbell was becoming a very familiar name to those empowered to vote for the Heisman Trophy Award.

The following week found the Longhorns on the road again, traveling to Dallas to play the unranked Southern Methodist Mustangs.

They still held their number two ranking because of an unbelievable show of force against each of two very powerful teams, Oklahoma and Arkansas. Southern Methodist was outmatched, but played a gutsy game nonetheless, losing 30-14. Once again, Earl had a huge day. He gained 213 yards on 32 carries, and scored another touchdown in the process. After this 200-yard game, there was no denying that Earl would be in the running for the Heisman, should God see to it that he stay healthy.

At this point in the '77 season, the Longhorns were on a roll, and the players were beginning to feel invincible. They prepared to confront another true test against the Red Raiders of Texas Tech, who were ranked fourteenth in the nation, in a game to be played at Memorial Stadium. Many of the Longhorn players were still smarting from the previous year's loss, and intended to show their displeasure with an offensive and defensive assault, the likes of which the Red Raiders had never seen. They followed through on their intentions, pounding the Red Raiders 26-0, helped in large part by Earl's 116 yards rushing on 27 carries. He simply wore the Red Raider defense down with each carry of the ball. Finally, after thrashing the Red Raiders, and for the first time since 1970, The University of Texas Longhorns achieved top billing in the country. They were clearly the team to beat.

Next stop for the mighty 'Horns was Rice Stadium, where they were pitted against the University of Houston Cougars. This was the game in which Coach Akers became a true believer in Earl, and where he came to understand the young man's desire to succeed against all odds. On the night before the match, as the team was reporting for a meeting, Earl complained that he wasn't feeling well and had been sick to his stomach most of the day. The team doctor was called in and discovered that he was running a 104-degree fever. He had obviously caught a flu bug during the week. Earl was immediately put to bed, where he spent the night shivering and sweating in a strange hotel room. The severity of the bug, and the combined effect of the medications he'd been prescribed, left him completely unable to sleep.

The next morning, Coach Akers and the doctor immediately went to Earl's room to see if he'd improved at all during the night. Earl was still running a 101-degree fever, but insisted that he was going to play. He remembered what had happened the previous year, and couldn't stand the thought of letting the team down again. Though the team doctor didn't think Earl should try to play because of the drain on his energy level, in the end he left the decision up to Coach Akers and Earl. To Earl, it didn't even matter what Coach Akers thought, because he was going to play no matter what.

Fred Akers did give Earl permission to play, and he played before the largest crowd ever to witness a Texas/Houston matchup.

"I was going to let it all hang out, so to speak, to see exactly what Earl Campbell was like on the inside," Akers remarked later.

He found out in a most remarkable fashion. Still running a fever, and with no food in his stomach, Earl riddled the Cougar defense with 173 yards on 24 carries, scoring three touchdowns in the process. On his second touchdown run, Earl went flying full speed into the corner of the end zone — where he promptly encountered Bevo, the Longhorn steer which serves as the school's mascot. In what became the first and only time known to God or man, Earl knocked a standing Bevo to his knees. The huge Longhorn easily weighed over eight hundred pounds, but in the end he was no match for the charging locomotive that was Earl Campbell.

Joyce Owens was sitting in that particular corner of Rice Stadium on that day, and proudly proclaims that she has one of the few pictures taken of this remarkable feat. The photo shows Earl kneeling next to the unsuspecting beast, who had literally been sent sprawling on all fours. This picture now sits in the Owens' summer home, where it makes for quite an unusual conversation piece.

The third touchdown Earl scored was on his last run of the day, a 43-yard blast straight up the middle. As he crossed the end line, Earl got down on his knees and raised both hands in the air. It wasn't an arrogant, conceited gesture, rather, it was confirmation by a very special, talented athlete that none of his incredible runs could have been done without God's help. The final score was 35-21 in the Longhorns' favor. Moreover, Earl Campbell had proven himself, beyond a shadow of a doubt, to an admiring coach and an equally admiring group of teammates.

The Houston game prompted Fred Akers, like many before him, to declare, "Earl Campbell is the greatest football player I have ever seen and Ann Campbell is the best coach there ever was!" Once again, strong words of admiration from someone who had spent most of his life watching football players mature.

Texas Christian was the Longhorns' next opponent at Memorial Stadium. The result was much the same as it had been the previous nine years, with Texas dominating the game, winning handily by a score of 44-14. Earl had what was becoming for him a typical day. He gained 153 yards on 21 carries and scored two touchdowns.

As soon as the game ended, all of the Longhorn players began looking forward to the following week, when Baylor, who had embarrassed them the previous year, would make a house call. This game was also to be televised nationally and would give Earl's teammates an opportunity to personally — and very publicly — hype their Heisman candidate.

As it turns out, the game wasn't exactly what Earl's teammates had in mind, because they came out flat; "deflated," was the way Rick Ingraham put it. The score was uncomfortably close, and the Longhorns took a 10-7 lead into the locker room at half-time. The third quarter was essentially more of the same, with the Longhorns constantly finding themselves trapped deep in their own side of the field. There was little evidence of a "fire in the belly" being shown by the nation's top-ranked team, and UT was definitely not impressing a national television audience hungry for, and accustomed to, that fire.

Finally, Rick Ingraham had had enough, realizing that if things kept going the way they were, the Longhorns would most assuredly lose their top ranking, and not only that, but Earl Campbell could possibly lose whatever edge he may have gained in his quest for the coveted Heisman Trophy.

As the team huddled in their own end zone, Ingraham, who knew full well that an entire country was watching his team falter, blurted four simple words: "Heisman Trophy, my ass." From that point forward, all hell broke loose, as Earl took the statement to heart and went on a one-man rampage, literally destroying any defender who dared get in his path. The final score was 29-7, and Earl finished with 181 yards on 30 carries, scoring a 43-yard touchdown for good measure.

Texas maintained their number-one ranking after the Baylor game and, as many analysts came to agree, the Heisman Trophy was boiling down to a three-man race. Two of the contenders were running backs. Doug Williams was having a huge year at quarterback for Grambling State. The numbers he was putting up each week were unbelievable, and he was sure to be a top choice for a lucky professional team. Terry Miller, a running back from Oklahoma State, was said to be neck and neck with Earl. It became apparent that the Heisman Trophy winner would be decided on how these players fared in their last regular season game. For Earl, it meant another trip to College Station for his last meeting with the twelfth-ranked Aggies.

It was to Earl's advantage that the Longhorns' Thanksgiving Day game against the Aggies was also to be televised nationally, the fourth such appearance in ten games. Everyone playing on and rooting for the Texas Longhorn football team was aware that the Aggies would be keying on Earl to ensure that he wouldn't embarrass them in front of an entire country. As Earl viewed it, "The time had come to deliver the goods."

As the teams were preparing to take the field for that most important, season-ending game, Fred Akers took Earl aside for a one-on-one conversation, out of earshot of everyone else.

"Mr. Campbell, do you *really* want to win the Heisman Trophy?" Akers asked, clearly baiting his one-man audience.

Earl convincingly replied, "Yes sir, I do. I want it real bad."

"Good," Akers responded. "You go out there and get me anything over 150 yards rushing, making every play seem like it's the most important of your life. If you do this, I feel certain that the award will be yours. Now go on out there and get it done!"

Akers commanded Earl to do this, completely aware that he could be wrong even if Earl did as he was told. The truth was that no one could accurately predict who the Heisman Trophy winner would be. Akers was also aware that The University of Texas didn't do much publicizing on behalf of the coveted award, other than in their media guide.

As Coach Akers viewed the situation, "If Earl was going to win the Heisman, it'd have to be done purely by the style of football *he* played."

There's one thing about Earl Campbell that people close to him have known all along: if someone whom Earl respects tells him to do something that makes sense to him, he goes out and gets it done, come hell or high water. After listening to Coach Akers' prediction about what it would take to win the Heisman, Earl went out against the twelfth ranked team in the nation and became a one-man wrecking crew. On Texas' very first offensive series, Randy McEachern rolled right, realizing that the hyped-up Aggie defense would be in an adrenaline-induced pursuit. He found Earl Campbell all by his lonesome out in the left flat. As was the case in the infamous Arkansas game, McEachern threw the ball to Earl and remembered saying to himself, "Please catch the ball, Brickhands, *please.*"

As it turns out, "old Brickhands" came through and scrambled 65 yards, untouched, into the A&M end zone. The stadium of over 80,000 hysterical Aggie supporters went deathly silent, and would be forced to remain that way over the duration of the game. On his last regular season game in a Longhorn uniform, and with a nation of turkey-filled people watching in disbelief, Earl gained 222 yards rushing on 27 attempts. He averaged a mind-boggling 8.2 yards per carry against the much heralded Aggie defense, and, in addition, scored four rushing touchdowns. And so it was that the Longhorns defeated their bitterest rivals, 57-28.

The 'Horns were now undefeated and won the Southwest Conference Championship outright. They had retained the number one ranking for five consecutive weeks, no easy feat considering how unpredictable the pollsters had been in previous seasons. In his first season as head coach of the Texas Longhorns, Fred Akers had taken those members of Darrell Royal's dream-team recruiting class and developed them into the champions they were destined to be.

Earl Campbell's career statistics at The University of Texas are staggering when put in proper perspective. He had gained 4,443 yards rushing in 765 attempts, an average of 5.8 yards per carry. What's more, he scored a Longhorn record of 41 rushing touchdowns, only three of which came in his junior season when he was hurt and missed five games. Sports reporters and watchful admirers alike were truly awed by the running abilities of this phenomenal athlete. Through it all, however, Earl kept these achievements in perspective. Always humble, he never lost sight of giving thanks to God for all He had done, and paying tribute to his mother for all she had done.

As expected, award after award was being bestowed upon Earl now. Earl was named to the All-Southwest Conference team and to the Bob Hope All-America Team. Unfortunately, he had a test the day after the Bob Hope show was to be taped, so he advised Hope's staff that he couldn't attend. Bob Hope personally called Earl to inform him that he would send a private jet to pick him up and fly him back that evening after the taping was finished. Once again, Earl had to politely decline Mr. Hope's gracious offer. He told him that he wasn't comfortable on airplanes and wouldn't be able to study under those circumstances. Besides, he couldn't risk the possibility of flunking the test. Mr. Hope understood and praised Earl for his commitment.

Fred Akers best summarized the stand Earl had taken on this issue, "Any other player would have missed the entire week to be on the Bob Hope All-America show. Not Earl. His principles were strong enough to say 'no' to a media legend, and be respected by that legend for doing so."

The still-unnamed Heisman winner was scheduled to be announced during the first week of December at the Downtown Athletic Club in New York City. As the day for the Heisman presentation grew near, one extraordinary statistic about Earl's performance kept appearing time after time, for all interested followers to see. 1977 was the first year that the Texas Longhorns kept statistics on what they termed, "Yards After Contact," or YAC. Once a person carried the ball and received an initial hit by a defensive player, YAC represented the amount of additional yards he was able to gain while carrying or dragging players with him. In the case of Earl Campbell, over 800 of his 1,744 yards rushing were made after contact! Even when analyzed by the sharpest of football minds, this statistic was nearly impossible to comprehend. It could only be truly understood by the unfortunate defensive players who found themselves in the path of The Tyler Rose.

Earl's biggest boost during the Heisman Hype was given by Ken McDermott, a writer for *People* Magazine. While covering an assignment in Houston, McDermott heard about all the unbelievable foot-ball feats young Earl Campbell was accomplishing at The University of Texas, and decided to do a feature story on The Tyler Rose for *People*. As is so often the case in an award such as the Heisman, any type of positive media exposure, especially in a world-famous maga-zine, leaves a distinct impression on those who vote. Again, God had provided the right person at the right time for Earl and, hard as it was for the young man to believe, this time it was a member of the previously reviled media.

The time had finally arrived for the Heisman Trophy to be awarded. Among the finalists were Earl Campbell, Gifford Nielsen of Brigham Young University, Terry Miller from Oklahoma State, Ken MacAfee and Ross Browner from The University of Notre Dame, and Doug Williams of Grambling State. Each finalist was given several invitations, along with complimentary hotel accommodations. Not surprisingly, Earl decided to take his mother. He also took Henry and Nell Bell, extremely close friends of the family, as well as little Louis Murillo, Darrell Royal, Brad Shearer (who by now had already won the Outland Trophy for the best defensive lineman in the country), and Rick Ingraham, now a close personal friend.

When the time came to leave the New York hotel for the Downtown Athletic Club, an enormous stretch limo was waiting. Earl ushered everyone inside except Louis Murillo, telling them that he and Louis would meet them at the Club. Then Earl hailed a cab.

While others might have been puzzled by Earl's refusal to take a limo to the ceremonies, Ann La Croix was very familiar with the reason. She later recalled, "Ever since the death of Earl's father, and the memories Earl carries with him, he has never been comfortable riding in a limo. Earl can't even look out the window of his car at a funeral procession that's passing by, *that's* how much the death of B.C. Campbell affected him so many years ago. So, if you're trying to figure out why he went to the Heisman in a cab, look no more. Earl simply can't tolerate anything that symbolizes death."

1977 was the first year that the Heisman Trophy Award was presented like the Academy Awards, with an extremely flamboyant setting for the nationally televised event. In attendance from the sports world, to present many of the various awards, was Reggie Jackson, who had recently been dubbed "Mr. October" for his outstanding effort in the Yankees' World Series performance that year. Also present was O. J. Simpson, who had gained over two thousand yards rushing the previous year for the Buffalo Bills.

Sitting at Earl's table was Louis Murillo, who had stayed by Earl's side all day to ensure that no harm came to his friend before they got to the ceremony. Also at the table were Rick Ingraham and Brad Shearer, who had obviously had no difficulty finding suitable stops among the plethora of bars that graced the hotels and streets of the Big Apple. As Earl fondly recalls, "By the time Rick and Brad got to the awards, they was feelin' no pain!"

To many it seemed that the night would go on forever, but finally Reggie Jackson took the stage to announce the winner of the award for "The Best Running Back in the Nation." Earl fervently hoped this honor wouldn't go to him, as that would most assuredly take him out of the running for the Heisman.

He soon learned that all his wishing was for naught, as Jackson opened the envelope and proudly proclaimed: "And . . . the winner is . . . from The University of Texas, Earl Campbell!" The audience erupted with applause, but Earl was in a state of mild shock as he climbed the stairs leading to the stage.

After he accepted the Crystal Award from Jackson, he mumbled a few words into the microphone — meaningless words, because Earl was hurt. In his heart he was thinking, "This isn't what I came to New York City for." As an escort led him backstage, Earl was still dazed and confused, not quite knowing which way to go to get back to his seat. It wasn't that he lacked gratitude, but the gratitude was overshadowed for now by his hurt and disappointment.

Then suddenly a voice came up from behind, saying, "You better get back to your seat; there's still another important award to be given out." Earl turned around to encounter O. J. Simpson, who led him out from behind the stage and back into the audience. When Louis, Rick, and Brad saw the hurt on their friend's face, they realized that Earl thought he was out of the running for the Heisman.

Earl was in such a fog that he barely heard Jay Berwanger, the first Heisman Trophy recipient, as he announced, "And now, the moment we've all been waiting for: the award for the most outstanding college football player in America."

While Berwanger was speaking, Brad and Rick kept reiterating to an as-yet-uncomprehending Earl, "Don't worry, you're gonna win the Heisman, too. Trust us, we can tell by the way the crowd's reacting."

The thunderous voice of the announcer once again filled the room as he finished opening the envelope. "And the winner of the 1977 Heisman Trophy Award for the greatest college football player in America is . . . " He paused for a few moments of maddening silence, further adding to the tension within the room. ". . . from The University of Texas, Earl Campbell!"

Earl was still in shock as Rick, Brad, and Louis began hugging him and slapping him on the back. But the shock that came over him now was good. No, it was beyond good; it was one that made him feel like shouting, "Look, Dad! Look what I've done, and I owe it all to you." As Earl began walking toward the stairs, shaking hands with many people he had never met, the orchestra began playing, "The Eyes of Texas." Earl felt a cold chill go through his body, knowing that Darrell Royal and The University of Texas had truly made this moment possible. After receiving the enormous bronze trophy, which displayed a football player with his right arm straight out in the famous "stiff-arm" position and the left arm firmly cradling a football, Earl stepped up to the microphone.

"Ya know, when I was a kid and I'd get in trouble, I'd always want to say, 'Hey momma, I'm in trouble.' So, 'Hey momma, I'm in trouble!' I don't know what to say! It took a lot of hard work, and I really can't just say thanks to just one person, because there's been so many people included in it. But I *will* represent what a Heisman Trophy winner should be. Thank you very much."

Watching Earl Campbell accept the Heisman Trophy was an exceptional moment for Darrell Royal. It filled him with pride, and was proof-positive to him of what any individual with the proper amount of respect, discipline, and willingness to succeed can achieve. Royal knew that Earl Campbell possessed these attributes as the result of one person: his mother. Without Ann Campbell's guidance during her son's climb up the ladder of life, there would have been no awards, no trophies, and no fond memories for people like Darrell Royal to carry with them.

There was still one more mountain to climb for the Longhorns, one that would surely serve as the ultimate climax to an already unforgettable year. This final obstacle was the Cotton Bowl, to be played against none other than the Fighting Irish of Notre Dame. The powerful Irish team entered the game ranked fifth in the nation. Thirteen players on their roster would eventually go on to play in the National Football League, among these, a sophomore quarterback by the name of Joe Montana.

Unfortunately, this game turned out to be *anti*-climactic. From the beginning, nothing seemed to go right for the Longhorns. The Irish arrived in Dallas ten days before the Cotton Bowl was to be played, but the Longhorns stayed in Austin until three days before the showdown. In Austin, they endured two straight weeks of inclement weather, which was highly unusual for this beautiful Texas city.

Consequently, they were forced to practice indoors. When the 'Horns finally did arrive in Dallas, they still couldn't practice outdoors because the terrible weather had moved north with them. Once again, they were forced to practice within the limited confines of a local gymnasium.

January 1, 1978, saw freezing rain pouring down on the Cotton Bowl during the early morning hours. Although the Texas Longhorns were a two-touchdown favorite, the entire team came out flat. Many players attributed this to their lack of effective practice time. They fumbled twice and had a pass intercepted in the first half. UT simply couldn't get out of their own end of the field. They also lost Earl's blocking back, Johnnie "Ham" Jones, to injury on the last play before halftime. The undefeated Longhorns had to accept being behind, 24-10, at the intermission.

The second half proved no different, as the 'Horns continually shot themselves in the foot, fumbling the ball during several key possessions. Earl still managed to gain 125 yards rushing, but he couldn't match the power of the Irish, whose running backs both rushed for over 100 yards. It was the most deflating day in many of these brilliant young players' careers, as Texas lost 38-10.

This was a shocking defeat at the hands of the Dan Devine-coached Irish. Fred Akers accepted full responsibility for his team's showing, even though he knew they had played far below their potential. Akers still believes that Texas had the best team in the nation that year, though he has long since accepted the loss. What Fred Akers will never accept is the final ranking that was given his team. Notre Dame, because of its victory over the top ranked Longhorns, was voted into the position that Texas had vacated. At the same time, Texas had to accept Notre Dame's pre-game ranking of fifth, a bitter pill to swallow for a team grown accustomed to being number one.

For Rick Ingraham and many other members of the 1977

Longhorn team, the memory of that cold January day in Dallas is a recurring nightmare that will never fade. When asked if he had any regrets about his years spent playing for the Longhorns, Ingraham pondered for several moments before responding, "Yeah, one. That we could have beaten Notre Dame in the Cotton Bowl, because there's not a day that goes by that I don't think about that game and the 'what ifs' . . . "

Earl finished the spring semester of 1978 with passing grades. Due to his grueling football schedule, he was still twelve credits shy of receiving his degree. He was still bound and determined to receive the degree, but the NFL draft was just weeks away. Based on his career statistics for the Longhorns, Earl believed that he stood a good chance of being taken high in the draft, a profound understatement consistent with the humility of a football great who refused to don the mantle of superstar.

Fred Akers reflects back on his initial coaching season and the Longhorns' accomplishments as a team. He knows that The University of Texas has reaped many benefits from Earl Campbell's having played there. The school's reputation soared in the eyes of the nation, and this, in turn, brought various recruiting advantages to which no dollar amount can be affixed.

Finally, The University of Texas gained national respect because of the character that Earl Campbell represented. Honest to a fault, and a man of his word, Earl always followed through on what he said. Most importantly, he managed all these fine qualities with a sense of humility. There was never an ego with Earl, no pretensions about who he was or what he had accomplished.

Earl Campbell left The University of Texas knowing that he had done The Eyes of Texas proud.

EARL CAMPBELL'S
PHOTO ALBUM

A young future Heisman Trophy winner, Earl at age 10.

Earl's beloved father, B. C. Campbell, in the U. S. Army, 1943.

Earl and youngest son Tyler pose with the man who brought
Earl into this world, Dr. Kinsey, and Mrs. Kinsey.

This was Earl's first "home," the first of many football fields
upon which he would play.

This man, Coach LeCroix, became Earl's mentor at a very important time in Earl's life. This picture was taken as John Tyler High School was leaving for the State AAAA playoffs in the Astrodome.

Earl, at age 18, carrying the ball against Austin Reagan in the 1973 State Championship game in the Astrodome.

Earl, encouraging his teammates, even at the sidelines, during the State Championship game.

A tired Earl Campbell leaves the field after scoring one of his touchdowns in the 1973 State Championship game.

Earl's #20 jersey is retired, and proudly hangs in the gym at John Tyler High School.

The dedication proclamation hangs in the gym as part of John Tyler High School's tribute to Earl.

Earl at the dedication of the gym at John Tyler, with three of his great coaches; (left to right): Corky Nelson, Earl, Coach LeCroix, and Fred Akers. March 2, 1979.

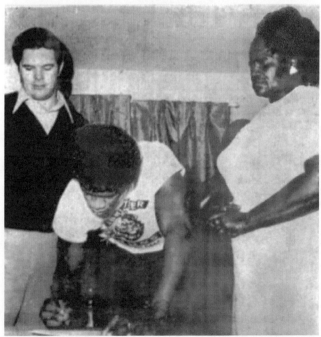

Earl signing his letter of intent to play for the Texas Longhorns, as his proud mother, Ann, and Coach Nelson look on.

Earl receiving one of his many awards from *Texas Football* magazine's Dave Campbell.

A proud Ann Campbell on the front porch of the old house after Earl had won the Heisman Trophy.

**Earl encouraging Johnny "Ham" Jones during a critical game
for the Longhorns.**

Earl running the ball against Texas Tech.

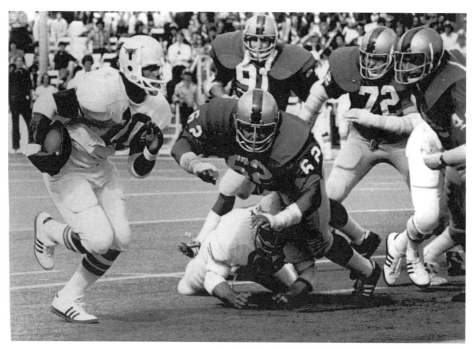

Earl carrying the ball against Boston College.

With Earl are All-American linebacker Tommy Nobis, Coach
Darrell Royal, and longtime friend Louie Murillo.

Earl receives his All-American honors from Bob Hope on his
1977 Christmas TV special.

Earl returns to Tyler after his playing days at The University
of Texas, and is presented with the keys to the city and a
parade held in his honor.

The award Earl worked so hard for, the Heisman Trophy, is displayed proudly in his mother Ann's home. He gave her the trophy as a token of his deep love and respect for her.

A recent picture of Earl and Coach Fred Akers, who provided Earl with the inspiration and guidance he needed to win the Heisman Trophy.

128

Ann Campbell, standing before the new home that Earl had built for her after signing with the Houston Oilers. The old house where Earl was raised stands to the right.

Earl and NFL Commissioner Pete Rosell at an awards ceremony in New York.

Earl (inset), Bum, and the Houston Oilers outside the Astro-dome.

Earl finally marries his childhood sweetheart after he begins his NFL career.

Earl poses at the altar with his six brothers, four sisters, and mother, Ann.

Two of the most loved men in Earl's life: Coach Bum Phillips (left) and Coach Darrell Royal.

Bum is the guest speaker at a 1987 dedication in Austin for Darrell Royal and Earl, where they were enshrined on the "Walk of Fame."

Earl currently has a very successful food business in Austin, Texas. Here, he sits in his office, surrounded by some of his many awards.

SECTION IV

"LUV YA BLUE"

OILER CANNONBALL

From sunny Miami, Florida, to icy
Boston, Mass.,
From the Broncos of Colorado, to
the iron in the Steelers mask.
He's mighty tough and rugged, He's
feared quite well by all.
He's the winning combination of
the Oiler Cannonball.
Here's to Head Coach Phillips,
May his name forever stand.
And always be remembered,
By the fans throughout the land.
When the Super Bowl is over
And those Cowboys finally fall,
We'll carry him home to Houston,
On the Oiler Cannonball.
Listen to the blockin', The ramblin',
and the roar,
As he glides along the sidelines,
By the hashmarks for the score.
From the fancy passin' dago, To the
Tyler bowling ball,
Those Patriots can be taken,
By the Oiler Cannonball.

Written by Carl Mauck

Houston Oilers center during the "Luv Ya Blue" era

Sung to the tune of WABASH CANNONBALL

"On the football field, Earl Campbell displayed an incredible desire for success. He took on the enormous responsibility of an entire football team and handled it with class, with dignity. Off the field, he had a definite understanding of his superstar status but **always** *remembered the way he was raised."*

Gifford Nielsen
Quarterback, Houston Oilers
1978-1983

"Luv Ya Blue"

It was an abnormally hot spring day in Austin, with the temperature rising well into the 90s by mid-afternoon. A few bluebonnets could still be seen on the wide lawns around the Capitol. Even though they were usually past their prime by this time, the early months of the year had been very rainy in the area, providing a long and late blooming season for the beautiful state flower of Texas.

Although this was to be one of the most important days in Earl's life, he did not stay home watching TV and waiting for the telephone to ring. He attended classes and did what was required of him, just as he had done on the day of the Bob Hope All-American presentation show a few months earlier. Most athletes with Earl's phenomenal senior-year athletic record would have been anxiously awaiting confirmation that they were one of the chosen few to be taken in the NFL draft. Not Earl. He was "business as usual," attending all his classes before heading home to the apartment that he and Alfred Jackson shared off campus.

Earl remembers his thoughts and feelings about the NFL draft and the draft day. "With the numbers I produced my senior year, combined with the Heisman, I figured I'd get taken in the draft. I really didn't care when I was taken, who took me, or how much money they were willing to pay. All I knew was that I wanted to play football on a professional level, to prove to everyone that awarding me the Heisman wasn't a fluke."

The phone was ringing when he unlocked the door.

A rather distraught Alfred Jackson was on the other end of the line. "Earl, where the heck you been, man? I've been tryin' to reach you for over an hour now. Are you aware what's happening in the draft?" Jackson, like many who'd been anxiously awaiting a phone call, couldn't believe his roommate's attitude on this very special day.

"Hey, Al, what's goin' on? I don't know about anything yet, 'cause I just got in from class."

The Tyler Rose: The Earl Campbell Story

"Man, haven't you seen the TV? You were taken *first* in the draft — number one, man! Best of all, you're gonna be stayin' in Texas, 'cause the Houston Oilers made some moves with Tampa Bay to get you. Man, are you lucky, 'cause you're gonna be playin' for Bum Phillips!"

Alfred was obviously much more elated than his always calm and composed roommate, and he was absolutely amazed when Earl responded, "Who?"

"Bum Phillips. You know, man. All his players *love* playin' for him 'cause he lets them be themselves. He lets them enjoy themselves *and* play the game at the same time. Man, Earl, there's a million other guys who'd just love to be in your shoes right now."

"Never heard of him. Is his name *really* Bum? If it is, I wonder what the players call him. Surely they don't call him Bum, do they?"

As usual, Earl was more concerned about how to address his new coach than about the details of the draft pertaining to him. Alfred laughed; manners were always so important to Earl, whether he was dealing with a coach, a professor, or any other older person.

"Say man, what did *you* hear from the draft?" Earl asked. Once again, Earl was concerned about the other guy.

Not once in their conversation did Earl get excited, talk about money, or brag on himself. All he was concerned about was proving himself on another level. He wanted the opportunity to show those who had voted for him that the Heisman was well-deserved. Being taken first in the 1978 draft was a definite vote of confidence by his future coach.

Earl had never met Bum Phillips and had no idea who he was at the time — but when these two personalities were finally brought together they would win the hearts, love, and confidence of an entire city. Without anyone being aware of it at the time, the "gestation period" for LUV YA BLUE began on the day Earl Campbell was drafted by the Columbia blue and white of the Houston Oilers.

"Luv Ya Blue"

If Earl had been aware of the maneuverings that had taken place behind closed doors in the draft to get the rights to him, he would have been much more appreciative of what Bum Phillips, Bud Adams, and the others in the Oiler front office had done. Knowing that Tampa Bay had the first pick that year in the draft, Bum called John McKay, head coach of the Buccaneers, on a whim. Bum knew that Coach McKay didn't need another top notch running back because he'd signed Rickey Bell to play for Tampa the year before. Bell had phenomenal numbers playing at USC, and had been considered a candidate for the Heisman Trophy.

Bum, on the other hand, knew he had something Tampa Bay was in desperate need of: a strong and powerful tight end with good hands for catching a football. He theorized that Jimmie Giles was the man for the job. He already had Mike Barber for this position, and reasoned that if he played it right, both teams could help each other. Even so, Bum didn't really believe that Coach McKay would give up the rights to Earl Campbell.

He nearly dropped the phone when McKay responded to his proposal by saying, "I'll have to clear it through Mr. Culverhouse." McKay, like Bum, always cleared such decisions with the owner of the team.

Bum regained his composure and said in the slow, methodical Texas twang that frequently belied his keen intelligence, "Please call me tomorra, 'cause we'll need to know one way or the other before too long."

When McKay didn't call the following day, Bum assumed he had come to his senses about the deal. What Bum didn't know, and wouldn't until the following day, was that McKay actually did try to contact him, but both Bum and Bud Adams were out of pocket and missed the call. The evidence of this historic draft swap had been scribbled on a message pad and left on the desk of a secretary — who had forgotten to give the message to the men when they came back into the office.

Now, with the Tuesday draft drawing ever closer, Bum once again called McKay. This time it was to confirm that Tampa was passing on the deal, seeing as how McKay had failed to call the Oilers back. He was shocked when McKay told him that he had indeed called back and had left a message. He added that he was equally surprised when Bum didn't get back to *him*.

Bum didn't have time to place blame or be angry, and that type of behavior just wasn't part of his laid back demeanor, anyway. Instead he made a beeline to Bud Adams' office to reconfirm that this was what Bud, as owner, wished to do. Bum always consulted with Adams before making a decision that concerned personnel, even though Phillips was the general manager of the Oilers as well as the head coach.

"Are you *sure* he's worth it?' Bud asked, fully aware that the price for a Heisman Trophy winner would undoubtedly be expensive. The decision had to be made quickly, because the ball was now in the Oilers' court for the draft swap.

"Heck yeah, I'm sure," Bum replied. "But I need to warn you, Bud, if we do get Campbell, it's gonna cost a lotta money to sign him, an' that's not gonna be where it all ends — 'cause once we sign him for a lotta money, your other players are also gonna want a whole lot more, and you're gonna have to give it to 'em!" Bum hoped to prepare Adams for where pro football was heading, with players' salaries escalating with each passing season. Tony Dorsett had set the pace the year before when he signed with the Dallas Cowboys.

Bud thought about Bum's last statement for only a few seconds before responding, "O.K., Bum, let's do it."

Being a businessman first, Adams knew the type of revenue Earl Campbell could generate on the Oilers' bottom line. Getting a native born Texan, a UT alumni, and a Heisman Trophy winner on the Oiler field would bring devoted and appreciative fans, and, more importantly to Bud, big bucks. Adams was right; Earl would pull in huge dividends at the ticket booth in return for his salary.

On the evening of draft day, Earl sat alone in his apartment thinking about the city where he would be playing pro ball. He also thought about his new coach, "Bum." The phone interrupted his thoughts. Earl knew that the chances were good that it was another call from another reporter, but that was okay, as he'd become more comfortable addressing the media after taking so many courses in Speech. He decided to take the call and make a few brief statements.

But it was not a reporter. When Earl picked up the phone and answered, "Hello" that evening, it would be his first taste of the man who would one day own a large part of his heart.

"Is Earl Campbell there, by any chance?" the voice asked, though it seemed to Earl that it took ten minutes for the person to get just those few words out over the heavy drawl.

"Speaking."

"Earl, this is Bum Phillips, head coach of the Houston Oilers. I'm just callin' to say 'howdy' on behalf of myself, Bud Adams, an' the team, an' to welcome you to our organization. I've already talked with Coach Royal, an' he says that you're my kinda people, so I know we're gonna have a lotta fun together, in addition to playin' some head-bangin' football. I just want you to know that if there's anything you need, jest gimme a holler, an' I'll get it done for you. If not, I'll see you next week when you come over to Houston to sign your contract. Once again, congratulations, Earl. I think we're gonna be good for each other."

Earl couldn't believe what he had just heard, because his coach sounded just like many of the East Texas people he had known all his life. All he could manage to say was, "O.K., Coach. I'll see y'all in Houston." When he hung up the phone, a huge smile crossed Earl's face, as the realization hit him that his new coach, this icon of professional football, was what is known in Texas as, "a good ole boy": friendly, and honest to a fault — not unlike Earl himself.

In point of fact, Bum Phillips *was* an East Texan, born and raised in Orange, a stone's throw from the Louisiana border. His manner of speech was obviously no 'put on,' because no one could convincingly fake these East-Texas colloquialisms.

Phillips had worked his way up the coaching ranks, starting with high school coaching. He eventually joined the San Diego Chargers as an assistant coach from 1967-1972. He followed his mentor, Sid Gillman, to the Oilers in 1974 as defensive coordinator. Gillman felt so strongly about Bum's coaching style that he convinced Bud Adams to offer Phillips the dual positions of head coach and general manager in 1975. Gillman took a position in the Oilers' front office, Bum took over his new posts, and history was on its way to being made.

Bum wasn't kidding when he told Earl that he had spoken with Coach Royal, for the two men had become friends over their years of coaching in the state of Texas. Royal was "tickled pink" upon receiving Bum's call with the news about Earl; he knew Earl would enjoy Bum's personality and that Bum Phillips would take care of his favorite athlete. Royal knew that Bum was a coach who didn't just look for athletes who could play football; he sought people of good character as well. In Bum's view, character was a necessity for winning. Coach Royal assured him that Earl had what it took to make the cut, and that the two of them working together seemed like "a match made in heaven."

With Coach Royal's word, Bum knew he need look no further for a star. Darrell Royal had long been known as a man of truth.

Bum was floored that Tampa Bay had accepted his trade request, especially when the Oilers were only required to give up Jimmie Giles, plus a first and third round draft pick. Bum looks back at this trade as the turning point in his own career.

"Luv Ya Blue"

In addition to capturing Earl, Bum considered himself fortunate to pick up Gifford Nielsen, a young quarterback from Brigham Young, with the Oilers' next pick. Nielsen was sixth in the Heisman balloting in his junior year, and was a strong contender his senior year, until he sustained a season ending knee injury in his fourth game. Despite this injury and the subsequent layoff, Bum was willing to gamble on Gifford. He believed that Gifford had what it took to play football for him, and that he had the requisite character. And once again, after the start of the season it became obvious that Bum's assessment was right on the money. Both Campbell and Nielsen proved to be gifted Oiler team players, who played with heart and sincerity.

The Oilers also picked up J.C. Wilson from the University of Pittsburgh as a cornerback. Wilson became an essential ingredient in the "smash-face" style of football that Bum was gearing his defense to play. Looking back, Bum realizes that the players he received from the '78 draft were truly a gift from above, for these young men would blend neatly with the seasoned veterans who were hungry for a championship.

Neither these veterans nor Bum Phillips knew that on the day he was drafted by the Houston Oilers, Earl Campbell made two deliberate and definite decisions. He knew, first of all, that he was going to build a new home for his mother to live in for the remainder of her life. And secondly, he knew beyond a doubt that he was going to be the best running back in professional football.

Earl flew into Houston Intercontinental Airport to sign his contract with the Houston Oilers, and was then taken by helicopter to the Oilers' practice field, located directly adjacent to their front offices on Fannin Street. As the helicopter landed, Earl couldn't help but notice a beautiful Columbia blue Lincoln Continental parked in the middle of the practice field. It was perhaps the nicest car he'd ever seen, with white leather interior complementing the soft blue paint of the exterior.

At the press conference, Bud Adams handed Earl the keys to this luxurious vehicle, in what Earl believed was a present for his signing with the team. Earl had no idea that it would be an omen of things to come in his relationship with the flashy owner of the Oilers.

Mike Trope, Earl's agent, had negotiated a contract with Bud Adams that contained a one and a half million dollar signing bonus, in addition to his yearly salary. After conferring with Trope, Earl elected to defer all but $200,000 of the bonus. This was an ingenious plan designed to pay him a yearly stipend well into his mid-forties. Although Earl understood the deferment of the signing bonus, once all of the paperwork was done he had no idea about what he was going to do with all of the money. It was simply more than his mind could comprehend.

To add to his confusion, Earl was being introduced to many influential people in front of the rolling cameras. It was, in fact, the first time Earl actually met Bud Adams, who made such a point of presenting the keys to that Continental when just the right camera angles were in place. Bum Phillips was also there to greet him. Earl took an immediate liking to the stocky man, who was dressed in jeans, western shirt, boots, and a big buckled belt. Bum was holding a large Stetson hat in his hand, a hat which he always wore to cover his block-shaped, crew-cut head. Earl would later come to learn that the reason Bum held the hat in his hands was, "'Cause Momma taught me never to wear my hat indoors."

And those were just a few of the unique personalities that Earl encountered on his first official day with the Oilers. He definitely wasn't in Tyler anymore.

Earl's signing was one of the biggest moments in Houston sports history, and was treated as such by the local radio and television stations. After Adams and Phillips had spoken to the press, Earl was hit with an avalanche of questions about himself and his style of play. He was interviewed by Dan Patrick, Ron Franklin, and Bob Allen from the local TV stations. With the confidence he had developed over the past few years, Earl answered all of the questions slowly, deliberately, and with respect — that is, until he was asked how it felt to be an instant millionaire. He had nothing to say to that question; the reality of what had happened to him just hadn't registered yet.

Despite his confidence, Earl still felt most comfortable when he was only required to talk about what he knew best: football. One reporter asked Earl who he would like to pattern himself after. True to his humble past, Earl thought briefly before answering, "I'm not gonna try to be Jim Brown, O.J. Simpson, or Tony Dorsett. I'm just Earl."

That remark convinced Bum Phillips once and for all that Earl was definitely his type of player, one not enamored of the glitz and glamour and bright lights of pro sports. "The man just wanted to play football," as Bum so succinctly put it.

After the cameras were turned off and the media left, Bum took Earl aside for a one-on-one conversation, the first of many. Bum liked to talk and he liked to philosophize.

A few minutes into their discussion Bum asked, "What're you gonna do with two hundred thousand dollars, Earl?"

"I dunno," Earl said. "I've never had this much money in my life, and didn't think that I ever would." The truth be told, Earl had never had a checking or savings account, and didn't even know much about what banks actually did.

At that point, Earl's new friend and mentor stood up and said, "Earl, follow me," whereupon they went across the street to the Fannin Bank and opened a checking account for the young man with an initial deposit of $200,000.

After this was handled, Bum asked, in his unique drawl, "You like barbecue, Earl?"

Earl's eyes lit up as he responded, "Heck yeah, I love it!"

Bum took Earl to The Swinging Door, one of his favorite eateries, where the two men enjoyed some of the finest beef and sausage in the entire Lone Star State. Bum drank a cold beer with his meal, while Earl, who'd never had alcohol in his life, drank iced tea. His momma didn't approve of drinking.

During the course of their conversation Bum asked, "Well Earl, now that you're a millionaire, what're you gonna do for an encore?"

Earl reflected on this question for a minute before responding, "I'll tell you what I'm *not* gonna do, Bum. I'm *not* gonna change my name to CampBELL." The reference was to the previous year's top draft pick, who had changed the pronunciation of his last name to DorSET, with the accent on the second syllable — rather than what he'd been called all his life, pronounced DORset.

With that, Bum let out an enormous belly laugh, realizing that his new protégé was a most unpretentious man with a quiet sense of humor.

After dinner with Bum, Earl headed back to Austin in his new Lincoln Continental, a million and a half dollars richer. He looked at the road ahead and gave thanks to God for all He had bestowed upon him, fully aware that it was now time for the ultimate test: the bright lights and prestige of the National Football League.

Three weeks after the signing, Earl was sitting in his apartment when the phone rang. It was Coach Phillips, who was about to introduce him to the harsh realities of professional football. Bum had already told Earl that pro ball was nothing more than a business and that it was definitely a show.

"Earl, this is Bum. Say, where's that Lincoln you drove back to Austin?"

Earl sensed some apprehension in Bum's voice. "It's out in the parkin' lot, Coach. Why?"

"Well, Earl, I hate to tell you this, but that wasn't a gift from Bud Adams. He says you either gotta pay for it, or give it back!"

Earl was floored. Anger flooded him when he realized that what Bud Adams had done to him was nothing more than just another "dog and pony show" for the media — and what's more, he had used Earl to do it.

"Tell him he can have it back, Coach. If I'd known that, I'd never have driven it back in the first place!"

Bum was embarrassed, both for Earl and himself, as he replied, "I understand, Earl. I believe you've made the right decision!"

When Earl reported to training camp, he was still nine credits shy of receiving his degree, but he fully intended to go back and finish the remaining courses. He still wanted to prove the naysayers wrong, and to fulfill the commitment he had made to Coach Royal, his mother, and himself when he first went to The University of Texas.

Before he could do that, however, he had to prove himself to his teammates and coaches. A few in the Oilers' camp had made it public that they were questioning just what was so special about this new million-dollar wonder. Earl spent the first week with the other rookies, going through basic coordination drills under the watchful eye of the coaches. One of these drills was simple in concept, but Earl had a difficult time mastering it. He was required to run forward around pylon cones without touching them, then run backward, reversing the route he had just taken. Oddly, when he was required to run backward, Earl had absolutely no coordination, and would fall flat on his butt time after time.

One of the assistant coaches became extremely concerned about Earl's lack of backward movement, and wasted no time informing Coach Phillips that there was a chink in the star's armor.

147

Bum listened to the frantic coach, but he took it all in stride. "If y'all think about it," he replied calmly, "we didn't draft him to go backward."

This was perfectly logical to Bum. Watching the young man with 36 ½-inch thighs struggle through the simple drill, Bum wasn't worried. In fact, the whole situation amused him, because he knew that a man with a natural, God-given body like Earl's could do, as Bum put it, "damn near anything he wanted to do. He coulda worked in the oil fields, coulda been a boxer, or done anything with the strength that he displayed. But Earl wanted to play football, and play he did! With most men, they *needed* to lift weights to become strong. Not Earl, he was already strong, just naturally. He believed in flexibility, and rightfully so, since speed and awesome licks were his trademark."

The other coaches apparently still weren't satisfied. They found another problem: Earl could not run a complete mile without stopping. After observing this several times, that same assistant coach went to Bum, truly perplexed that the Heisman Trophy winner couldn't complete this simple exercise. He reported the bad news to Phillips, certain that this time the team leader would be duly concerned.

Instead, Bum looked at his assistant and smiled, "That's all right. We just won't give him the ball on third down and a mile to go!"

Although he was concerned, Earl knew that everything would be fine once he took his first hit. As he put it, "Runnin' and agility drills never were my bag, if y'all know what I mean." Those who eventually faced him on the gridiron would fully understand just exactly what he meant.

At the beginning of his first week in Houston, Earl moved into the Paseo Apartments, a complex close to the Oiler facilities. Upon finding this out, a cousin of Earl's, who also lived in Houston, was furious that Earl had chosen a less than desirable neighborhood without consulting her first. Accordingly, she found a condominium for him in a more upscale neighborhood, and he leased the penthouse. This, in his cousin's eyes, was only appropriate for his new station in life.

Earl's first order of business was to ask J.C. Wilson, whom he had taken a liking to when he met him, to move in with him. J.C. didn't know the city either, nor did he have a place to stay. It was only natural for the two newcomers to strike up a friendship.

That next Sunday, the veterans reported to camp with an enthusiasm and determination that Bum hadn't seen in them before. The reason was simple. They realized that if their new rookie sensation could perform nearly as well as he did in college, they would finally have a running game to complement the deadly passing attack of quarterback Dan Pastorini. Contrary to what Earl originally believed about needing to prove himself to them, these veterans were *hoping* he would succeed, as they truly believed that all the ingredients necessary for a Super Bowl were now in place. All they asked of Earl was that he live up to the salary the front office was paying him.

If there was any initial envy or resentment of the newcomer, these feelings were offset by the judicious influence and remarkable team-building skills of Bum Phillips. Gifford Nielsen recalls that Bum had "a unique ability to break down all barriers between the players, bringing them together as a team in the process."

Bum would often preach to his men, "If y'all will just do it my way, we're gonna be successful." The players soon came to believe this, and they also came to believe in the abilities of Earl Campbell. Within the first few days, Earl's laid-back personality permeated their ranks, as they began singing country songs before practice and during stretching and calisthenics.

Nielsen believes that before "Luv Ya Blue" was adopted by the fans, it came to life during the second week of practice, when the personalities of Bum Phillips and Earl Campbell merged to become one driving spirit. These personalities were downright infectious, and many of the players began dressing in western clothes just like Bum and Earl.

Houston was primed and ready for a sports team such as the Oilers were becoming. This new team gave rise to an excitement and pride that the city had never experienced before, and probably will never experience again, at least not from the blue and white of the Oilers. It was truly a most amazing bond between players and fans.

There was no mistaking that team and fans alike sat up and took notice when Earl finished the preseason, leading the league in rushing, with 265 yards on 47 carries. Optimism prevailed, due at least partly to the Oiler victory over the Dallas Cowboys, widely regarded as "America's Team." The starting combination of Giff Nielsen at quarterback and Earl Campbell at running back shocked the Cowboys as well as the viewing audience. With this win over the Cowboys, all the players and coaches on the Oiler team felt that something quite extraordinary was happening within their organization.

And then the time finally arrived for "Bum's boys" to make a statement to the nation. Their regular season opener was played against the Atlanta Falcons, and what a statement they made. Although the Oilers lost, 20-17, Earl Campbell would no longer be looked upon as a highly paid question mark; he gained 137 yards on 15 carries, on one of which he sprinted for 73 yards and a touchdown.

Earl's performance prompted Atlanta coach Leeman Bennett to state, "I was hoping that if we got to him early, he'd cough the ball up like a lot of young players do. But we hit him, hit him, hit him, and he never fumbled. He's going to be an exceptionally good NFL back."

Many of the Houston supporters, including the media, were ebullient but still leery, because they had seen the Oilers make strong starts before, only to drop in the ratings toward the end of the season. Not to worry; after Earl's next game in Kansas City against the highly regarded Chiefs, the unmistakable feeling of victory was in the air. *Luv Ya Blue* was really taking hold now.

In this game, Earl ran for 111 yards on 22 carries and scored two touchdowns. One of these scores was the game winner on a two-yard dive, with only one minute remaining in the game. The final score was 20-17. The media finally admitted in print that there *was* a difference with this Oiler team. The truth behind what appeared in print was that Houston had a winner because the team believed in themselves, and that was where it all had to start.

After the second game against the Chiefs, Bum called Conway Hayman into his office. Conway was a 6'3", 295-pound offensive lineman out of the University of Delaware, who was playing in his seventh season with the NFL.

Bum told the lineman, "Connie, from this point forward, Earl is gonna be your roommate on the road and your responsibility. As a favor for me, show him the ropes, 'cause I know he'll be in good hands with you."

Bum knew that Conway was a devout Christian, like Earl, and the coach wanted to make sure that no one, especially any of his players, steered Earl in the wrong direction. Of course, Bum also knew he would have to answer personally to Ann Campbell if anything bad happened to her Earl. Bum trusted Conway because he knew that he would accept the responsibility and that Earl would learn and develop, not only as a player but as a man, under Hayman's tutelage.

It is true that Hayman possessed all of Bum's character requirements, but there was one variable that Bum may not have counted on. Earl was still a young prankster at heart, and, like all good pranksters, he unveiled it in the most unexpected ways. First there were the candy bar capers. As Conway soon learned, Earl would not eat anything but Snickers™ Bars the night before, and during the time

151

leading up to, a game. Earl developed a peculiar habit of waking Conway up in the middle of the night to go find some of his favorite candy bars. Though he had given Bum his word that he would watch over Earl, Conway sometimes wondered if he weren't being asked to go above and beyond the call of duty. He swears that Earl would purposely not buy any Snickers on the way from the airport, just so he could wake Conway up at all hours and send him on a candy quest.

But that wasn't the extent of Earl's mischief. Earl had another peculiarity: dipping snuff. He'd gotten in the habit of filling several Styrofoam cups just a quarter of the way up with his snuff juice, and then placing them strategically around the hotel room as Conway slept. When Conway awoke in the middle of the night and headed for the bathroom, he would inevitably run into Earl's snuff traps. Earl would feign sleep, but Conway says his charge would be under the covers, giggling like a child and thoroughly delighted with his latest prank.

There were many times when Conway questioned why he'd said yes to Bum's request to be Earl's guardian, but deep down inside, he knew that he'd walk on hot coals for either of them.

During each week of the season, Earl and J.C. Wilson would sit at home and study films of their upcoming opponent's games, looking for any weaknesses that could possibly give the Oilers an edge. As they went through this ritual before their first game against Pittsburgh, they knew they had their work cut out for them. Neither Earl nor J.C. could spot many deficiencies in the Steelers' attack.

Earl and J.C. knew well how important their game with Pittsburgh would be, because the Oilers/Steelers game would be televised on ABC's Monday Night Football, allowing the Oilers the opportunity to showcase their talents nationally. The team sported a 5-2 record at this point. As they prepared for the Steelers game, both young men realized that they would have to be running on all cylinders. The game was being played in Three Rivers Stadium, and Pittsburgh rarely left any margin for error, especially in front of their ardent home-town fans.

The hitting in the game was ferocious, on both sides of the ball. But Chuck Noll and the Steelers just weren't prepared for the awesome display of power that Earl gave the nation that night. He rushed for 89 yards on 21 carries, and scored three touchdowns. The last of these touchdowns was the game winner, with ten minutes left on the clock. The final score was 24-17, and the Oilers flew home to Houston a victorious team — not just in spirit but in the standings as well.

Their record had now improved to 6-2, midway through the season. Both the fans and media were now believers. A winner — and, more than that, a winning spirit — had finally emerged in a city starved for a champion. The ultimate proof of this new spirit was to come to Houston in the Astrodome on another Monday night, in a game against the Miami Dolphins.

The day after the Pittsburgh game, Earl signed the paperwork for the purchase of his first house, with the help of his cousin. The house was located on Candle Lane, in an elegant neighborhood in southwest Houston. To Earl and J.C., it was breathtaking. They moved in the same week the paperwork was signed.

What Earl wasn't aware of was that he and J.C. were the only blacks in the middle of a predominantly Jewish neighborhood. Earl found this out in a rather embarrassing way when he went out to his driveway that first week, and saw a dark-skinned man walking down the sidewalk. Earl had lived a sheltered life growing up in Tyler, and honestly believed that a white man was white and that a dark-skinned man was either black or Hispanic.

Earl, trying to be as friendly as possible, said to the elderly gentleman, *"Que paso?"* which means, "What's happening?" in Spanish.

The man immediately turned and addressed his new neighbor, "I don't know who you are talking to, young man, but I am of Jewish ancestry."

Earl raced back into the house to tell J.C. what had happened, and to discuss how amends could be made to their new acquaintance. He found out later that day that they were the only blacks on the entire street. Remembering his first misguided efforts at being neighborly but really blowing it, Earl broke into a full-faced smile. His Jewish neighbors eventually came to genuinely like and respect these two big men, and their children often visited Earl's house to listen to stories about playing football in the National Football League.

In fact, Earl became so appreciated by his neighbors that they tried to get the street renamed to Campbell Lane. Kathy Whitmire, Houston's mayor at the time, blocked all attempts to do this. The name has remained Candle Lane, though in spirit, the street is Earl's.

November 20, 1978, was to be a night that Earl and the city of Houston will never forget. This was the game in which the Oilers would be facing the revered Miami Dolphins on Monday Night Football, and it would be the formal coming out party for the fans' "Luv Ya Blue" mania. The Oilers were entering this game with an 8-3 record, and if they were able to maintain the course they were on, would be sure contenders for the AFC Central Division Championship. Howard Cosell and Frank Gifford were announcing the game for ABC. As the spectators entered the Dome, everyone was given a pair of blue and white pom-poms.

Earl remembers three things about that game. He remembers Reuna sitting in the first row behind the Oiler bench on the fifty-yard line; this was the seat she occupied for all of the Oiler home games. He remembers the pom-poms being shaken in unison by the fans in the sold-out stadium. But most of all he remembers the noise.

"Luv Ya Blue"

The fans who'd been fortunate enough to get a ticket were in rare form. ABC Television started their introduction to the game by showing replays of Earl's performance against the Steelers on the huge Astrodome screens; the responsive cheers began low but grew as each successive play flashed on. To Earl, it seemed the fans no longer had faces. They had become a sea of waving pom-poms moving with the cheers.

"It was absolutely deafenin'," Earl recalls. "Before the game, it was obvious to all us players that the fans had truly taken us into their hearts and made us a part of them. At that moment in time, the players and fans became one."

Gifford Nielsen, who was loosening his arm on the sideline, remembers, "This was the game where Luv Ya Blue was finally born, after many months of tentative hoping by the fans. The entire team could feel, by the reaction of the crowd, that we had something very special on offense and defense. The fans fell in love with the effort the team put forth and made us part of their lives, mainly because of Bum Phillips and Earl Campbell. But make no mistake about it, the fan pride of Luv Ya Blue was *earned;* it definitely wasn't just given!"

Conway Hayman also recalls that Luv Ya Blue burst into full bloom at the Miami game. "To put it simply, Luv Ya Blue was the ultimate approval given by the fans to the team, in particular, Bum Phillips and Earl Campbell."

Earl says, "The display of Luv Ya Blue was a chance for people of all races and backgrounds to come together as a city. More than that, it was a *feeling* that the players and fans shared without even talkin'." As is his nature, Earl finished by stating, "We owed it all to one man: Bum Phillips."

The game itself started with a fevered intensity. The Oilers were fueled by their newfound marriage with the fans, who maintained their deafening noise level throughout the duration of the game. Earl was exhausted after each play, and he seemed to take

155

forever to get back up and into the huddle again. Tim Wilson, his blocking back, was truly concerned after one particular play where Earl got walloped by several Miami Dolphins. It was his twenty-fourth carry of the night and, after Earl finally got back to the huddle, Wilson could see him gasping for air from the bruising play. His tongue was literally hanging out. Earl was so much in need of air that he didn't hear the play that was called, which was going to be a pitchout to him.

When he turned around to look at Earl, Wilson could tell he hadn't heard the play. He fully intended to call time-out for Earl to recover and get the signals straight. Earl shook his head, reading what was on his mind. With that, Wilson yelled at Earl, "Just follow me."

His concern was further intensified when Earl yelled back, "What's it on?"

With great trepidation, Wilson held two fingers behind his back for Earl to see. When Pastorini took the snap, Earl followed his teammate around the right side, taking the pitch in the process. Instead of cutting inside, which was what he had been doing most of the night, Earl chose to go out, breaking numerous tackles and outrunning the swift defensive backs in an eighty-one yard sprint down the sideline for a touchdown. As he crossed the goal line, Earl dropped the ball and got down on his knees, thanking God for giving him the strength to run that play.

The Oilers went on to defeat Miami, 35-30, in what Howard Cosell would later proclaim to be the greatest football game he had ever broadcast. Cosell's sentiments were mirrored by many others when the Houston/Miami matchup was voted the most exciting game played in the first twenty-five years of Monday Night Football's existence.

Earl finished the game with 199 yards on 28 carries, scoring four touchdowns. To this day, the memory of kneeling in the end zone, with the frenzied fans screaming and shaking their pom-poms, remains etched in his mind. After that game, people in Houston and the national media began referring to the team as the Houston *Earlers,* paying homage to the definitive personality the rookie sensation had given to the team. It was a kind of cowboy personality, one that was low-keyed yet forceful, accentuated by good manners and a deep-rooted sense of humility.

The city of Houston was on fire, and a man named Bum Phillips was pouring fuel on a flame called Earl Campbell.

Many members of the media began to question whether Bum Phillips might be abusing his rookie running back by calling upon him to run the ball so frequently. When Earl saw this in the newspaper, he remembered what an unfriendly press could do to a coach. He recalled the unfair and biased media coverage given to Darrell Royal when playing for The University of Texas.

Earl immediately went to bat for Bum by openly stating, "This perception of abuse on my running abilities is definitely wrong. In fact, I *want* the ball thirty times a game. I'd be upset if it didn't turn out that way."

Bum took the accusations in stride and addressed them in his mild-mannered style. "Many of y'all have questioned my use of Earl Campbell, since it's obvious that it takes him longer than most players to get up off the ground. That's true! But did y'all ever notice that it also takes a long time for Earl to *go down* on the ground?"

Bum's logic was mirrored by Dan Pastorini, who defended both Bum and Earl when the media questioned him about the coach's alleged overuse of Earl. Pastorini told the press, "Even when Earl comes back to the huddle walking on his tongue, he still wants to carry the ball. I'll ask him how he is, and he always says everything's fine. I've just about stopped asking, because he keeps giving me the same answer."

And if Pastorini's backing of his coach and teammate weren't enough, many opponents started to defend Bum's use of Earl as well. Such was the case after the Oilers played the Los Angeles Rams. Their defensive safety, Bill Simpson, had this to say to the media, "Tackling Earl Campbell is like tackling a runaway train. He got tougher as the game went along, and that's the true test of a running back!"

The Oilers finished the regular season at 10-6, losing to the Steelers at home in their last game, and in the process losing a shot at the division title. They earned a wild card invitation to the playoffs, but would be forced to go on the road for each of their games. It was the first time in nine years that the Oilers had made it to the playoffs. The players gave credit for the good season, in part, to the loyalty of their fans — but the fans gave credit to the strength of the team, the amazing performance of Earl Campbell, and the guidance of Bum Phillips.

Their first playoff game was played in the Orange Bowl against the Miami Dolphins, the team Earl had almost single-handedly beaten before a national television audience. Once again, the Oilers played their tails off and came away victorious, 17-9. Earl had 84 yards on 26 carries, and scored one touchdown in a brutally hard-hitting match. To say the least, he was sore on the plane ride home, but the thrill of a playoff victory put the pain in the back of his mind.

The following week, the Oilers traveled to Foxboro, Massachusetts, to play the highly regarded New England Patriots. The Patriots were heavy favorites to win, based on their 11-5 season record and the fact they were playing at home. Once again, the Oilers proved their doubters wrong with a 31-14 pounding of the Patriots.

The win prompted Raymond Clayborn — Earl's ex-teammate at The University of Texas, now playing for the Patriots — to say: "The one doubt that I had about Earl was that because he's so big and strong, he'd try to run over everybody, and I wasn't sure he'd last very long. Well, the way it's turned out, he's not hurt. He's doing the hurting!"

In the New England game, Earl had 115 yards on 27 carries with one touchdown. The plane ride home was filled with electricity, for the players had no doubt now that they had earned their way into the AFC Championship Game and "rubber match," to be played against their arch-rival, the hated and dreaded Pittsburgh Steelers.

As the week leading up to the Steeler showdown progressed, virtually every store, home, and automobile in Houston and Harris County was brandishing a Columbia blue and white "Luv Ya Blue" sign. Bumper stickers proclaimed it, and many people used soap and polish on their cars to show their loyalty to, and faith in, the team.

Earl was fully aware that the Steelers' defense was referred to as "The Steel Curtain" because of their no-nonsense, smash-face style of play. Their unspoken leader was Mean Joe Greene, a defensive lineman who ate running backs like candy. Given all this, Earl found it remarkable that both the Steelers and Oilers, though fiercely competitive on the field, never "talked trash" during the game. Although the teams were enemies on the field, each respected the other.

Beyond Mean Joe Greene, the Steelers had a formidable lineup. There was Mel Blount, whom Earl rightfully regarded as the best defensive back in the league. At 6'2", 210 pounds, Blount was tall and strong, and Earl had a very difficult time using his trademark stiff-arm on this skilled veteran. The Steelers also had Terry Bradshaw as quarterback, a player the media liked to poke fun at because of his laid-back Louisiana speech patterns. Bradshaw was, in fact, a fierce competitor with the most powerful throwing arm Earl had ever seen.

There was no doubt in Earl's mind that "to beat the Steelers on their home turf, we're definitely gonna have to earn it!"

The game was played on January 7, 1979, in what has come to

be known as "The Ice Bowl." All morning before the game, sleet fell on the field, while the temperature dipped to near zero.

Conway Hayman firmly believes that the Oilers became too preoccupied with the nasty, cold conditions before the game even began, and that the Steelers had an advantage because they were more accustomed to playing in freezing weather.

But Bum made no excuses, because, as he said, "Both teams had to play on the same field."

The bottom line was that the Steel Curtain dominated the Oiler offense from the start of the game to the finish. Earl was held to 62 yards on 22 carries in a 34-5 thumping, certainly not the game the Oilers had been hoping for. In addition to the weather factor, it is also noteworthy that Pittsburgh had won two Super Bowls in a row with the same team they fielded that day. Earl gave much-deserved credit to the team the Steelers had put together, and made no excuses for himself or his teammates.

As Bum reflects back on that Steeler team, "Pittsburgh had such a great team that if they decided they needed to win it (the game), they'd just go out and win it." These thoughts did little to lift the dejected Oilers as they met with Bum in the locker room.

Characteristically, Bum told his team, "Men, win or lose, as long as y'all gave it your best, that's all I've ever asked of y'all." They had, indeed, given it their best, under the worst possible conditions, and Bum knew it. He only hoped that each man would look at the whole season and not just this last game. Bum understood that if they surveyed what they had accomplished as a team, each player would find the pride needed to overcome defeat and to learn from it.

To add to the misery of the Oiler team and coaches, their flight was delayed three-and-a-half hours because of the bad weather. Waiting at the Pittsburgh Airport wasn't exactly high on their collective wish list. They were a defeated and exhausted team, and they still had a lot of traveling ahead. Once they landed in Houston, they'd still have to board a bus at Intercontinental Airport in Houston, and then head to the Astrodome, where their cars were parked, to finally get home.

What the players *didn't* know, as they finally boarded that jet in Pittsburgh, was that there were 50,000 screaming Luv Ya Blue fans waiting inside the Astrodome to welcome them home. Thousands of Houstonians in their cars lined the streets around the Dome, just to show their love and support for their team who had worked so hard to win a championship for them and their city.

When they finally arrived back in Houston and boarded the buses for the trip to the Dome, Conway Hayman was the first to observe, "Hey, there're no cars on I-45!" This was unusual, as this freeway is normally one of the most traveled and congested highways in the city of Houston.

When the bus driver heard Conway, he turned and grinned, "Yeah, that's 'cause the cops blocked all the entrances. We're the only ones on the entire freeway."

As the buses neared the Dome, the players noticed the large number of cars parked along the sides of the street. Some had loyal fans standing on top of their hoods holding Luv Ya Blue signs and shouting their appreciation for *their* team. As the bus slowly made its way to Fannin Street, the crowd of fans was even greater. Some ran alongside the bus, waving and screaming at the players.

And they hadn't even gotten to the Astrodome yet.

To say that the players and coaches were moved by this show of appreciation would be an understatement. This was something that none of them, including Bum, had been expecting. As they entered the stadium gates, there wasn't a single empty parking space in the huge lot. The players realized that because of the delayed return flight, these fans had been there for over four hours. There had been speeches made, cheers screamed, and faces painted blue. Bands played, and many Houston leaders sang the team's praises. This was a pep rally that had to be seen — no, experienced — to be believed.

Outside the entrance to the Dome, Earl was asked to get off the bus and sit on the back of a police motorcycle. Bum, Dan Pastorini, Carl Mauck, and Mike Barber were in a limo that they had boarded at the airport. As the enormous stadium door rose to let the Oilers' vehicles in, Earl heard what he describes as, "the most earth-shattering noise I'd ever heard."

Earl remembers that as he began his descent down the ramp onto the floor of the stadium, "an immediate chill went up and down my spine. The noise in the Dome was so loud that I couldn't even hear the roar of the policeman's motorcycle engine, and all I remember seein' were the pom-poms. They were everywhere, man, and I got real choked up inside by the gratitude displayed by the fans. It was somethin' I'll never forget. There was no doubt in my mind, or any of the other players and coaches, that Luv Ya Blue *was* for real. It wasn't a silly slogan that somebody thought up. It was for *real*."

Dan Pastorini recalls, "Even inside the limo with the doors closed and the windows rolled up, we couldn't hear each other speaking."

The famous Derrick Dolls, Houston's cheerleading squad, were engaged in a continuous rendition of the Oiler fight song. Each time the song ended, the place would go crazy, and the Dolls would start it up again.

"Houston has the Oilers,
They're the greatest football team.
They take the ball from goal to goal,
They're the best you've ever seen.
Houston Oilers, Houston Oilers,
Houston Oilers, number one.
Luv Ya Blue."

"Luv Ya Blue"

Over and over the simple song was sung, each time with increased frenzy, until all the coaches and players had finally gotten out of the vehicles and had begun waving to the standing-room-only crowd. Microphones were set up for those who wished to speak. Earl chose not to address the crowd.

When Bum Phillips took his place at the podium, there were visible tears in his eyes. The stadium became deathly still as Bum mulled over what he was going to say to this crowd of supporters.

Finally, the words came. "This year, we knocked on the door. Next year, *we're gonna kick that sumbitch in!*" Only Bum Phillips could sum up the thoughts of the team so concisely. Once again, the walls of the Dome shook with the cheers from the fans. For the Oilers and for all of Houston, it was an extraordinary night.

Though the '78-'79 season ended with the Pittsburgh Steelers reigning once again as Super Bowl Champions, Earl's accomplishments during the season did not go unnoticed and unrewarded. He received numerous accolades from the league, as well as from players and coaches he'd played against. He won the rushing title in his rookie season by gaining 1,450 yards on 302 carries, an incredible average of 4.8 yards per carry. He was voted Rookie of the Year, and Most Valuable Player of the National Football League. He was also named as an All Pro selection, and received his first of many invitations to the Pro Bowl.

Needless to say, Earl had more than proven that he had been the rightful recipient of the Heisman Trophy the year before. More importantly, he had proven to himself that he could indeed play football at the professional level, and play well. But Earl still wasn't satisfied, because he and his teammates still didn't wear the symbol of their ultimate goal: a Super Bowl ring.

When asked what he thought about his many awards and accomplishments, Earl stated to the press in his usual humble manner,

The Tyler Rose: The Earl Campbell Story

"I'm just a guy who believes that if you work hard enough, some rewards will come your way. I've tried to work hard. That's all!"

Bum Phillips gave credit where credit was due when he said, "Earl Campbell is the best runnin' back who ever put on a pair of shoulder pads. He always got better from his twentieth carry to his thirty-fifth, 'cause by then he'd done hammered 'em down!"

Never one to be at a loss for words, Carl Mauck, the Oiler center, described the feelings of those who had to block for him. "Earl's mother did a great job raising him. Heisman and all, he came in here humble and with a great attitude. As a person, he can't be beat. As a football player, the thing about him is that if you give him the same hole that you'd give another back, he'll always get more yardage on the play. He hits the hole quicker too, so you don't have to hold a block as long. And because we know he can break a run and go all the way, it makes us block a little harder for him."

What more need be said? Luv Ya Blue!

In the spring of 1979, Earl returned to The University of Texas and completed the necessary requirements for a Bachelor's Degree in Speech Communications. He tried to do this with as little fanfare as possible, even though he was aware of his national notoriety. He just wanted to be like any other student and do his work. He elected not to attend the commencement ceremony because he didn't want to focus attention on himself when so many other students deserved recognition for their hard work and commitment. Besides, he had proven to himself that he could achieve academically as well as athletically. That, in itself, was reward enough for Earl.

In the summer of the 1979 season, Earl met another NFL superstar living in Houston, Charlie Joiner of the San Diego Chargers. Charlie was fleet of foot and had an excellent pair of hands when it came to catching a bullet thrown from a quarterback's hands. Being aware of Earl's talents, Charlie asked the NFL's newest superstar if he'd like to work out with him under the direction of his personal trainer, Tom Williams.

Williams was from the old school, much like Frank Medina. He asked no fee for his services, feeling that watching the athletes progress according to his schedule was payment enough. His basic requirement was that they listen and work hard. Williams didn't believe in lifting weights; he developed his athletes by running and flexibility exercises. When Earl heard about the trainer's unusual techniques, he agreed to work with him. It had long been established that he didn't need weight training because of his God-given strength and mass. He did need some work on long-distance running and flexibility, if only to appease Bum's critical assistant coaches.

Both Earl and Charlie worked out with Williams three times a day, and when Earl reported to training camp that summer, he was undeniably in the best shape of his life. The assistant coaches could rest easy, as their star could now run a mile with ease — as if it really mattered. Earl himself felt better about it and about his whole physical being. *That* mattered.

Bum was fielding much the same team as the year before, with a nucleus of perhaps six true football players that could make the cut on any other team's roster. The rest were overachievers, whom Bum had convinced to believe in themselves and their abilities. They achieved and they won, and that's what mattered most. The only real difference between the 1978 season and the one starting in 1979 was that the fans were already believers, and Luv Ya Blue was a fact, not merely a hoped-for ideal.

In the Oiler front office, Bud Adams had hired an accountant by the name of Ladd Herzeg to be his Chief Financial Officer. The original plan was for Herzeg to have little or nothing to do with the day-to-day operations of the team, especially in relation to personnel and Bum's relationship with Bud Adams. Earl and Bum soon came to realize that this was not to be.

Over the course of the season, Herzeg convinced Adams that Bum's popularity had far surpassed his (which it had), and that everyone looked at the Oilers as "Bum's Team." It wasn't that Bum had set out to win a popularity contest; it'd just happened that way. But Herzeg was able to convince Adams that he was going to have to do something about it, and the relationship between Bum and Adams began to deteriorate.

Fortunately, Ladd Herzeg's manipulations in the front office did not disturb the Oilers or their coach on the field. They had another phenomenal year, with an 11-5 record during the regular season. Once again, however, the Steelers stole Houston's season-ending thunder, as well as their chance for the AFC Central Division Championship, by going 12-4, thereby claiming rights to the crown. As a repeat of the 1978 season, the Oilers had to face their nemesis at Three Rivers Stadium after defeating Denver 13-7, and San Diego 17-14. This time, the weather didn't prove fatal to the Oilers. It was the officiating that was their greatest adversary.

One particular call against the Oilers would be disputed for years, and changed the entire momentum of the game, which ended with a final score of 27-13. In the third quarter, the boys in blue were holding their own, but trailing 17-10. They found themselves going in for a score with the ball on the Steeler six yard line. Dan Pastorini lofted a pass deep into the right corner of the end zone, and wide receiver Mike Renfro snared it as he was sliding along the back line. The officials ruled that Renfro had not kept his feet in bounds as he caught the ball, thereby nullifying the touchdown.

Bum and the others frantically disputed the call. The protest, however, was to no avail, and the Oilers had to settle for a Toni Fritsch field goal. Their momentum broken, the Oiler offense was held scoreless by the Steel Curtain for the remainder of the game. Once again, they had to settle for second best in the AFC.

"Luv Ya Blue"

To those faithful fans watching the game in Houston, there was no doubt that Renfro was in bounds when he caught the ball. The catch was replayed hundreds of times, and each time, the knowledge that the team had been robbed by bad officiating stung anew. There was never an apology from NFL headquarters regarding the call, and none would ever come. This time, the taste of defeat was all the more bitter, since it was delivered at the hands of an "unbiased" (perhaps inept) third party, rather than by a superior team.

After this gut-wrenching loss to the Steelers, the plane ride home was much more subdued than even the previous year's, the pain of losing amplified by the nullification of the Renfro touchdown. Earl felt especially defeated; the Steel Curtain had totally shut him down, and he had only managed to gain 15 yards on 17 carries.

Bum declared that he'd "live a lot longer if I didn't have to play against Pittsburgh three times a year." As a matter of fact, he says he wants this statement engraved on his tombstone.

As in the previous year, the loss to Pittsburgh was a little easier for the Oilers to take, once the players and coaches got to the Astrodome and their loyal Luv Ya Blue fans. This year, the fans were in even more of a frenzy because of the Renfro call. They displayed their pride and vented their anger by tearing down the fence around the parking lot, in order to get closer to the entrance more quickly. Many of the players feel that the atmosphere inside the stadium was even crazier than in 1978, as a loss to Pittsburgh was difficult enough to accept without also having to accept the fact that victory was stolen from them by lousy officiating. For the second year in a row, the Oilers had given everything they had to their Houston fans, and the fans knew it.

With this second consecutive conference championship loss to the Steelers, Ladd Herzeg gained fuel for his campaign against Bum Phillips. Herzeg was able to sway Ed Biles, the Oilers' defensive coordinator, to see his point of view.

Biles rode to work with Bum daily, and professed to be his friend. Through Biles, Earl later discovered Herzeg had also solicited Greg Bingham, the Oiler middle linebacker, who began playing "both sides of the fence," becoming a snitch for Herzeg and Biles against Bum and the rest of the team.

Herzeg's strategy to rid the Oilers of Bum was devious. He'd report to Adams that Phillips, as a coach, had gotten too close to his players and had lost his effectiveness. Herzeg accused Bum of being more like a father to the team than a coach. It was true that Bum did many things no other NFL coach did, such as throwing pizza and beer parties for the entire team on a weekly basis, and allowing the players' families to attend practice the Saturday before a home game. What Herzeg and Adams failed to realize was that Bum did these things not to make himself appreciated as a father figure, but rather, to build team morale and team spirit. In short, he did them to be a good coach.

Bum's response to these ridiculous allegations was simple: "Heck, I'm awful close to *my* momma, too. I know that she loves me, but she also disciplines me. I believe that bein' close to my players gives me a distinct advantage 'cause they play for money, but they *also* play for the kinship they have with their teammates."

One can't help but wonder how Bud Adams could possibly side with the dissenters, in view of his team's two consecutive trips to the AFC Championship. But somehow Herzeg, Biles, and Bingham found a way to appeal to Bud's megalomania and win him over.

At the conclusion of the '79 season, Pittsburgh claimed another Super Bowl ring, but once again many awards were bestowed on Earl. For the second consecutive year he claimed the rushing title, gaining 1,697 yards on 368 carries, for a 3.6 yard per carry average. He also led the league in touchdowns scored, with 19. And once again, he received The Most Valuable Player Award, was named All

Pro, and was selected to the Pro Bowl.

Earl believes that these awards are a result of the positive influence Bum Phillips had on him as an athlete and as a man. He states proudly, "I know how much football knowledge Bum had, and as a person or as a coach, I'd walk the plank for him."

Two very significant events happened to Earl during the '79 season, events that he'll never forget. In a game against the Oakland Raiders, Earl took the hardest hit he had ever received in the game of football from Jack Tatum, the Raiders' defensive back, who was universally regarded as the toughest hitter in the league. Tatum collided with Earl at the Raider one yard line, in a hit that Dan Pastorini said was so loud, "It sounded like a train wreck."

After absorbing the full force of Tatum's blow, Earl fell backward into the end zone, got up on one knee, and realized, since he was still conscious, that he had just "beaten the best." Jack was rather glassy-eyed from the experience too. Though they got off to a jarring start, to this day Earl and Jack Tatum remain the best of friends, their friendship borne of a deep mutual respect.

The second, and completely devastating, event which shaped Earl's life that year was the sudden and unexpected death of Lawrence "Butch" La Croix, who dropped dead from a massive heart attack while Earl was attending training camp. Although Earl told Ann La Croix that he couldn't make it to the viewing or funeral because of training camp, Mrs. La Croix knew the real reason.

"Earl simply couldn't handle burying someone who had become another father to him, not at that stage of his life."

On February 12, 1980, Earl was ill with the flu and had been confined to bed by his doctors. Many of his Jewish neighbors and friends checked in on him, some bringing bowls of their home-made chicken soup to speed his recovery. Earl remembers that as he lay in bed, simultaneously shivering under the covers and sweating profusely, he received what he feels to have been a directive from God.

Earl recalls: "[I realized] it was time to propose marriage to Reuna, because I truly loved her and she had done so much for me, unselfishly, in the past." That night, the fever broke. The next morning, weak as he was, the first thing he did was go to a jewelry store and purchase an engagement ring.

On February 14, 1980, Valentine's day, Earl drove to Tyler, unannounced. He went to see his mother first at her new house, which he had built the previous summer. As he drove up in the driveway and looked at the brick house, Earl smiled to himself, glad that he had been able to make good on his promise. When Ann Campbell saw her middle child walk through the door, she was surprised.

"Hello, Earl. What brings you back to Tyler?"

"I forgot somethin' here, momma."

"I see. And what might that be, son?" Ann asked, truly perplexed at his response.

"I forgot Reuna, momma. I'm in love with her and I'm gonna marry her. I just wanted to let you know first, before I go over to propose." As was his nature, Earl wanted to follow the proper protocol and tell his family first.

Ann cried when she heard Earl's gentle proclamation, having known for years that he and Reuna were meant to be together. She immediately gave Earl her blessing; Reuna, she told him, was such a giving and caring person that she had always been first in Ann's heart for Earl. Ann knew that Reuna had never loved anyone but Earl.

Earl then went over to the home of L.G. Smith, Reuna's father, knowing that Reuna was still at work. Both Reuna's mother and father were surprised to see Earl, since they usually knew of his arrivals in town, well in advance.

"Mr. Smith, I've done a lot of thinkin', and I really love your daughter. I'm here to ask for her hand in marriage, with y'all's blessin' and permission, of course."

"Are you sure, Earl?" L.G. asked. "After all, she's been my responsibility for all these years, and it's my duty to see she is taken care of. Are you sure you're *ready* for marriage?" L.G. knew that Earl had surely been offered many temptations during his young life.

With no hesitation whatsoever, Earl responded, "Quite sure, sir. The time is right!"

"Fine, then, son. You have our blessing. Just take care of our little girl."

"You can count on that, sir. I'm gonna do that."

Earl had no doubt that he was making the right decision. It was time to settle down, and he knew he could provide well for Reuna; she would never have to work again, unless she wanted to. He knew to his core that a life spent with Reuna, who had never wavered in her devotion to him, would be blessed.

When Reuna arrived home, she was naturally shocked to see Earl. But shock turned to joy as he proposed to her in front of her smiling parents. She accepted his proposal without hesitation, and cried when he put the ring on her finger. Her dream had come true: her knight in shining armor had finally come to take her away from the land of roses.

Earl and Reuna were married on May 30, 1980, in front of one thousand witnesses. In attendance were many of the role models who had helped mold Earl throughout his life, especially in his football career. Corky Nelson, Darrell Royal, Fred Akers, Bum Phillips, and many more were at the ceremony to acknowledge the love Earl and Reuna had for each other. The huge wedding party drove to the reception in Ernest Owens' customized Trailways bus, while the bride and groom's families were ushered in limos.

Earl was so proud of Reuna on their wedding day, just as he

had always been, and, it must be noted, he was grateful to her for carrying a bouquet of plain flowers and *not roses*. The following week, Reuna resigned from her nursing job in Tyler, joining Earl in the house on Candle Lane, and the Luv Ya Blue family in Houston.

Many important changes took place in the Oiler camp during the off season prior to the 1980 opening kickoff. During one of the Oilers' last regular season home games in 1979, Dan Pastorini had been hurt, and had to leave the field in obvious pain. Many fans doubted whether his injury was real, and booed as he went over to the sideline. Pastorini's feelings were deeply hurt by this insult, as he felt there should be no doubt in anyone's mind that he had always given his best for the Oilers. Disillusioned and disgusted, he demanded that Bum trade him after the season.

Bum tried desperately to talk Dan out of leaving, but Pastorini was adamant. A swap was made with the Oakland Raiders to send Pastorini there, in exchange for Ken Stabler, "The Snake." Although Stabler was well known as a party animal off the field, Bum respected him as a team player, and felt he would fit nicely into the Oiler family.

In the trade, Bum also sent a package of future draft choices to Oakland to acquire tight end Dave Casper. Many people, including Ladd Herzeg, felt Casper was past his prime and loudly expressed their displeasure with this acquisition to Bud Adams. Herzeg felt that Bum had given the farm away to acquire an old horse. Bum obviously felt differently, and made the trade only with Bud Adams' "blessing." But this move would ultimately be the final nail in Bum Phillips' coffin as head coach of the Houston Oilers.

As it turned out, the season proved that Dave Casper still had the "win at all costs" attitude Bum was looking for. Ladd Herzeg, naturally, saw the situation differently. The Oilers finished with an 11-5 regular season record. They particularly relished knocking their arch-rival Pittsburgh Steelers out of the playoff picture late in the season, with a 6-0 victory at the Astrodome. The down side was that the Cleveland Browns claimed the AFC Central Championship, which meant that the Oilers would once again be a wild-card seed in the post season.

Bum's boys traveled to Oakland in the first round to play a powerful Raider team. To the total surprise of the team, coaches, and fans, the Oilers were soundly beaten, 24-7. Earl had rushed for 91 yards on 27 carries, scoring the only Houston touchdown of the game.

With the sudden end of the 1980 season, there was no huge Luv Ya Blue reception at the Dome.

The dream had ended too quickly.

Being dealt cards from the bottom of the deck by a stranger is difficult to swallow, but being dealt cards from the bottom of the deck by a friend is even worse. This was the situation as Earl saw it at the time. He feels that Ladd Herzeg had effectively shut down all lines of communication between Bum Phillips and Bud Adams. Earl knew that Bum could deal with that, but when his supposed friend and defensive coordinator, Ed Biles, and then his middle linebacker, Greg Bingham, turned on him, his fate was sealed.

Earl found it very difficult to be part of a team where Bum was having to deal with personnel who had become Benedict Arnolds for their own gain. There was no doubt in Earl's mind that Greg Bingham was playing Ed Biles' fair-haired boy to increase his chances for continued playing time with Biles at the Oiler helm. Biles' inducement was similarly transparent to Earl: Biles wanted to be a head coach in the NFL, and he would do anything to anyone to get there.

Neither Adams nor Herzeg could deal with the fact that Bum had become a hero to the people of Houston, his popularity far surpassing that of his boss. With Bum's key people working against him, his questionable draft choices to Oakland, and the uncommon closeness he had with his players, it was inevitable: Ladd Herzeg was finally able to convince Bud Adams that Bum Phillips had to go.

In what has become known in Houston as "The New Year's Eve Massacre," Bum was called into Bud Adams' office on December 31, 1980, and fired as head coach of the Houston Oilers. And so it was that the man who had directed his team to two consecutive AFC Championship games in a row, and a first-round playoff loss the following year, was suddenly unemployed. (Oddly enough, all the teams who had beaten the Oilers during this three year span went on to win Super Bowls.)

Bum took Adams' news like the big man he was, telling his ex-boss, "Bud, I told you the day that I took this job that someday you'd be firin' me, an' when you did, I'd shake your hand, then thank you, and leave. Well, thank you for the opportunity, I wish you luck." That said, the laid-back cowboy stuck out his hand and shook Bud's hand.

Bum knew that Adams would *need* some luck with the Oilers now that he, Bum, was being drummed out of a job. The fans in Houston were not going to like the fact that he was fired or how he was fired. Bum knew that Adams was going to have a tough row to hoe, and couldn't help but chuckle to himself at the thought.

The media and the people of Houston were incensed when the news hit. Instead of enhancing Bud Adams' popularity, the firing of Bum Phillips validated what Houston fans had thought for some time now: Bud Adams was, to put it mildly, not a "people" person. To Earl, he was just an old moneybags, out for only the almighty dollar. It had become obvious that Adams didn't care about the team or the city.

Bum, on the other hand, was devoted to his team and his city, and during the seven years he coached in Houston, the fans took him into their hearts as one of their own. He still is.

Bum never really had a chance to say good-bye to the players. He was hired as head coach of the New Orleans Saints on January 2, 1981, just two days after Bud Adams fired him.

"Luv Ya Blue"

"Things weren't all that bad," Bum recalls. "Heck, I went from a $174,000 a year job (with the Oilers), to one that paid me $450,000. Plus, on the second day I was there, they (the Saints) gave me an $8800 Rolex watch. Shoot, I worked for Bud Adams for seven years an' he never even gave me the time of day. *That's* the difference between the two organizations. Bud Adams actually did me a big favor."

Bum Phillips took with him many fond memories of his time in Houston, especially the Luv Ya Blue era that began its decline the day he was fired. Even today, when Bum talks about those days, he can't help but get emotional.

"It all started with an exceptionally good group of kids, 'cause I picked 'em. I wanted guys who cared about each other, and about their responsibility to the public. I wanted players who the fans would feel comfortable with, players who would willingly go to the children's hospitals every week, people who the fans could literally embrace. You see, this was around the time the movie 'Urban Cowboy' was released, an' it was filmed in an' around Houston. Since I'm a pseudo cowboy, always dressin' like one, it was great that my players followed suit.

"I guess the true meanin' of Luv Ya Blue was expressed by the *people of Houston,* who came to embrace the team 'cause of how hard they tried. In my boys, they saw people who ain't never quit in a ballgame. That's what I guess Luv Ya Blue meant to me."

In 1989, the players and coaches from the Luv Ya Blue era reunited for a charity golf tournament. Of the 93 ex-players from that time, 89 came to the reunion. This was particularly remarkable because by then the players and coaches were scattered throughout the country. But it didn't strike Bum as being the least bit unusual, because he knows that, "That's just the kinda group they are!"

The Tyler Rose: The Earl Campbell Story

When Earl Campbell found out about the firing of his friend and coach, he reminded himself that professional football was nothing more than a business whose bottom line oftentimes counts more to an owner than a win-loss record, or the feelings of fans or a city. Even so, the firing was difficult for Earl to accept. He experienced once again that tremendous sense of loss resulting from having another father figure removed from his daily existence. He looked back with sadness to all the great times that he and Bum had shared with the Oilers, and would never share again.

Never did it cross Earl's mind that something like this could also happen to him, since he firmly believed that he was going to retire from professional football as a Houston Oiler.

The 1980 season was Earl Campbell's most productive year in professional football. For the third year in a row, he led the league in rushing, gaining 1,934 yards on 373 carries, for a mind-boggling average of 5.2 yards per carry. He was once again voted All Pro and was a Pro Bowl selection. Earl's 1,934 yards gained on the ground marked the third highest ever produced in the NFL. To achieve these numbers, he had rushed for over 200 yards in a game four times, and over 100 yards eleven times. Only one team was able to hold him under 100 yards rushing that year. Because of this, he was named the Most Valuable Player in the National Football League for the third consecutive year — and this was only the third year he had played professional football.

Prior to the 1981 season, Ralph Wallace, a member of the Texas State Legislature, introduced a resolution proclaiming Earl Campbell to be an Official State Hero of Texas. The resolution passed, and to Earl's surprise and slight embarrassment, he found himself ranked in the same category with the only three other gentlemen in Texas history to be so honored: Stephen F. Austin, Davy

Crockett, and Sam Houston. Earl was the first person in over 150 years to be given this most prestigious honor. He was humbled as Texans everywhere expressed their thank you to a man who was the epitome of a model Texan, representing the Lone Star State throughout the country and the world.

1981 was a year of drastic change for the Oiler infrastructure. Ed Biles was, to nobody's great surprise, named head coach, following the script written and dictated by Ladd Herzeg. Herzeg was named the new General Manager. His plan had worked, and the overly ambitious man saw his three-year scheme come to fruition. Ken Stabler announced his retirement, but was called back for the first game because Gifford Nielsen, the team's new starting quarterback, had suffered a devastating shoulder injury.

As Earl saw things taking shape, there was no doubt that Luv Ya Blue was a thing of the past. First off, Earl had taken an immediate dislike to Ed Biles as head coach. Like many members of the Oiler squad, he had no respect for Biles, believing he was the reason for Bum's dismissal. Earl resented Biles' propensity to single players out just to embarrass them. He seemed to take delight in making his players uncomfortable while he showed them that he was the "new sheriff in town." Earl had never respected anyone who elevated themselves at others' expense.

"It was a helluva change, goin' from somebody you really respected to havin' his supposed best friend come in and tear down everything that had been built upon in the past," Earl remembers.

Earl particularly disliked the fact that Biles removed the tried and true "I" formation, destroying a most productive rushing backfield in the process.

When all the dust settled that year, the team finished 7-9, and did not make the playoffs. Earl pulled his fair share of the load, rushing for 1,376 yards on 361 carries, and scoring ten touchdowns for the Oilers. He was once again voted an All Pro and selected as a member of the Pro Bowl team. But to Earl these awards were meaningless. They were tainted by the sight of his team going straight downhill.

1982 saw the NFL stymied by their first ever players' strike against the league and owners. Because of the strike, the season was limited to nine games. Coach Biles released Ken Stabler, and announced that Gifford Nielsen would be his new starting quarterback. After only one game, Biles reconsidered his decision and traded for Archie Manning. The Oilers finished with a dismal 1-8 record.

Earl, along with everyone else, felt the negativism that permeated the team. Although 1982 was a much shorter season, he still managed to finish with 538 yards rushing on 157 carries. He was selected All Pro and went to the Pro Bowl for the fifth consecutive year. But it seemed the dream was really over, for by this time, Oiler fans had once again become accustomed to the way the team used to be, before Bum and Luv Ya Blue: boring and lifeless.

By 1983, when the Oilers had racked up ten consecutive losses to begin the season, even Bud Adams finally realized the immense *faux pas* he had made. After the sixth loss, he'd finally seen enough, and he fired Ed Biles. At the time of his dismissal, Biles had compiled an 8-23 record in his two-and-a-half seasons as head coach. Chuck Studley was named as interim coach, taking the team to a 2-8 record during his tenure.

Archie Manning and Dave Casper were traded to the Minnesota Vikings after only three games, and Gifford Nielsen was left to pick up the pieces. Unfortunately for this very skilled quarterback, there were too many pieces in this puzzle to be picked up, and Giff suffered through seven consecutive losses before re-injuring his shoulder. Earl saw Oiler morale hit an all time low, and he wondered about the "what ifs" had Bum Phillips been allowed to remain as head coach of a now-crumbling team.

As for Bum, he was in "hawg heaven" in New Orleans. He inherited a 1-15 record from a losing team in the 1980 season and, in 1981, led his team into the Astrodome for a 27-24 upset over the once proud Oilers. The victory was bittersweet, because he still had many friends left on the Oiler squad. When the huge scoreboard flashed the words "Luv Ya Bum," the crowd in the dome went berserk, and the beloved coach stood, humbled and proud, in the outpouring of affection from his thousands of fans.

Over the course of his three seasons with the Saints, Bum had a 16-25 record, including the strike-shortened season. To Bum, the most important event was the Saints coming within two seconds of making their first playoff bid in 1983. They lost to the Los Angeles Rams on the last play of the game.

Although the Oilers had suffered through a terrible season, and despite the loss of his beloved coach, Earl was still producing the numbers. He finished the season with 1,301 yards on 322 carries with twelve touchdowns scored. He was selected as All Pro and Pro Bowl candidate for the sixth consecutive year.

As the 1984 season approached, Bud Adams made numerous changes, changes that he promised would have a positive effect on the performance of the team. First, he went north into the Canadian Football League and took as his new coach Hugh Campbell, of the Grey Cup-winning Edmonton Eskimos. Campbell brought with him a strong-armed young man by the name of Warren Moon to be his starting quarterback. Moon came with a huge price tag attached, one that angered many of the players on the Oiler roster, including Earl. Granted, Moon was good, but he was unproven in the NFL.

Earl believes that Hugh Campbell and Warren Moon "were a

package deal, from jump street."

Earl realized something very early in the season: "It was either Warren Moon's way or the highway. From the very beginnin', Warren started to tell me how to do things, like hit a certain hole, or make a block. I figured, 'who was this guy from the Canadian League to be tellin' me my assignments?' After awhile, I would just tell Warren to 'shove it.' I guess that was a mistake, but how was I to know that he'd turn out to be a snake in the grass?"

Earl soon found out exactly how much power Warren Moon had, although the revelation came in a manner that he certainly wasn't expecting. The day was October 8, 1984, and Earl had just finished taking his son, Christian, for a haircut. They were driving down Old Spanish Trail, near the Astrodome, headed for a Popeye's Chicken for lunch. Father and son were both enjoying the music of country radio station KIKK, when the disc jockey, Barry Warner, suddenly cut in and announced: "We have just received word that the Houston Oilers have traded star running back Earl Campbell to the New Orleans Saints for a first round draft pick. Campbell will be reunited with his old friend, Bum Phillips, head coach of the Saints."

In a state of shock, Earl pulled his car off to the side of the road. He could not believe what he had just heard. After the full reality of the announcement had sunk in, however, he was fighting mad. To learn about the trade in this manner was downright insulting.

Earl knew by now how the game of professional football worked, having witnessed first hand the firing of Bum Phillips. But this was different, because it was happening to *him*. He'd had no clue that negotiations for his trade were even being considered, or that management was in any way dissatisfied with his performance.

After all, he reasoned, "one of the four State Heroes of the State of Texas doesn't get traded without notification and the opportunity for an explanation." So he'd thought, anyway.

Earl has no doubt that Warren Moon played a major role in

his being shipped out. There was really no logical reason for the trade; Bum and the Saints already had George Rogers, the superb rookie running back out of South Carolina. To Earl, it seemed that Warren Moon, the "new kid on the block," didn't feel there was enough room under the spotlight to fit both superstars. That being the case, and with Moon's friend Hugh Campbell making decisions as head coach, Earl was the logical choice to be sent packing.

Fortunately for Earl, he didn't have a whole lot of time to brood over the trade, since he was due in New Orleans the following day. This was hardly the way he had envisioned saying good-bye to Houston and the Oilers.

That night, Earl emptied his locker, alone, after everyone had left for the day, wanting this quiet time to reflect about the good times and the bad times with the Oilers. He thought about the past six-and-a-half years he'd spent as an Oiler, and decided that the good times far outnumbered the bad. He remembered all the accomplishments the Oilers had achieved together, as a team, and he felt proud.

These days, Earl Campbell views the Oilers' current situation with mixed emotions. "Jeff Fisher fits today's standards as a coach. He can relate to the younger players and, if they (the Oilers' front office) will leave him alone, he's on the right track toward rebuildin' the team."

The very length of Earl's statement about the current Oilers is a clue for fans about how deeply affected he is by the situation. Earl still never talks much, and doesn't easily share his feelings with the public. "Unfortunately, Bud Adams has pulled yet another 'power play' that he's been so well-known for throughout the years. He firmly believes that the Astrodome is too small for his team to play in and intends to move the team to Nashville, Tennessee. Bud's mistake there was makin' everyone aware of his intentions instead of keepin' his mouth shut and simply moving out, if that's what he wanted, much like the owner of the Seattle Seahawks intended to. But then, Bud's been known for puttin' his foot in his mouth every time he says something related to football."

Earl continued, "Who I *really* feel for is the people in Houston, those who are caught in the middle of all this. Because of what he's already said and done, Bud has no choice but to pull the Oilers, since the people have lost all respect for him and how he chooses to do business. If the Oilers *were* forced to play in the Dome, they would be lucky to draw five thousand people per game. Just like Ed Biles, once you lose that respect, there's no goin' back to claim it again. *That's* why the men who I played with will always be remembered in Houston. Our respect was *earned*, something Bud never learned about, even with all his money."

SECTION V

NEW ORLEANS:
THE LAST HURRAH

The Tyler Rose: The Earl Campbell Story

"Earl Campbell is one of the truly genuine people I've come across. He doesn't know the meaning of the word 'I'. With Earl, it's always 'we' or 'us'."

O. A. "Bum" Phillips

Earl Campbell left Houston in a storm of controversy and arrived in New Orleans the same way. Houston fans felt he had been unfairly traded, and didn't like the backhanded, clandestine tactics behind the trade. New Orleans fans felt too much had been given away in the trade for this "over the hill" player.

Whatever the case or the city, Earl was not happy with the controversy and the ensuing media criticism. He felt that too much attention was being focused on him as an individual player, when the focus should be on the team effort, in whichever city he was playing football. Something essential was missing from his game when he arrived in New Orleans to play for the Saints and Bum Phillips; he had lost his passion, and no longer had that "fire in the belly" which had propelled him to stardom as a Longhorn and as an Oiler.

Even though Earl would now be back playing with his friend and mentor, Bum Phillips, and several of his former Oiler teammates, he was acutely aware that the fans didn't like him and would not accept him. They thought Bum was bringing over too many Oilers, especially since he had given away a first round draft choice to obtain Earl. New Orleans questioned Bum's need for Earl when the Saints already had George Rogers, a respected, top-notch running back.

All aspects of the Campbell trade had gone against the logic of the New Orleans fans. Media and fans alike felt that Earl was past his prime. In his many years of playing raw and bruising ball, the press implied, Earl was bound to have lost a step or two. In addition, the fans didn't understand why Bum decided to have Earl split playing time with George Rogers, instead of having Earl be the backup to their rookie sensation.

New Orleans: The Last Hurrah

Things were not going well for Earl, and the tension weighed heavily on him.

Despite the many negatives going in, Earl finally decided to set his mind to the task at hand, vowing to give his all for Bum once again, no matter the circumstances. The first order of business was to block out all of the critical media hype. Earl felt that he could focus on the game he so dearly loved to play, if everyone would just let him do his job and do his best.

Fortunately, some of the old fire returned. As had been the case several times in Earl's past, once he took his first lick on the field, the desire factor clicked in and drove him to excel. He finished the '84 season with 468 yards rushing on 168 attempts and four touchdowns. It wasn't the type of year he had hoped for or had achieved in his previous six years in professional football, but he felt good about his efforts.

His positive feelings were reinforced when Bum decided to trade George Rogers at the end of the season, openly proclaiming that Earl Campbell was, once again, "The Man."

But with the news of the Rogers trade, the media and fans turned on Bum and proclaimed their fury openly. To them, it seemed obvious that Bum was trying to establish a *"Luv Ya Blue"* type atmosphere in a city that just didn't want it. New Orleans fans had never made that unique connection with their many losing football teams.

The Saints franchise had been in existence for seventeen years, but the team had never been to a playoff game. Determined to end this disgraceful record, the media and fans issued a harsh ultimatum to the executive management of the Saints: "Bum either wins a playoff spot this year or, *Bum can get gone!*" But it was a Catch-22 situation, for without fan or media support, this would prove a most difficult task for Bum and his players to achieve.

The Tyler Rose: The Earl Campbell Story

As the 1985 preseason ended, Bum Phillips was having a difficult time understanding the negative attitude the New Orleans fans and the press held toward him. He was doing his best with what he had, and doing it without the help of either the media or the fans. The media were key, for Bum realized that he would never gain fan support without positive media backing, but this seemed unlikely in "The Big Easy."

After the Saints' first preseason loss at home, and continuing throughout the season, one disgruntled female Saints fan would stand above the tunnel the players and coaches had to go through to get to the locker room after the game. She was waiting for Bum Phillips, and when he got to just the right spot she would pour an ice cold sixteen-ounce cup of beer directly on top of his head. Because he still held fast to his momma's teachings about not wearing a hat indoors, Bum didn't even have his Stetson to protect him.

Bum couldn't help but notice that this fan never went after any of the players or other coaches, just him. Before too long, though, he figured out that she only got him with the beer when the Saints lost. So if he wanted to stay dry, he would just have to win every home game.

As it turned out, Bum had a wet season in '85, and the players had a long one. They were 4-8 after the first twelve games. Bum received three beer showers for the three home losses. After the third time, following a 27-3 loss to Seattle, Bum dried his sticky head and remarked, "That lady is never gonna have a chance to do that again." No one paid much attention to the remark, or what he meant by it — no one, that is, except for Earl Campbell. *He knew.*

After the Saints pulled off a stunning upset of the Minnesota Vikings in Minnesota, Bum had time to do a lot of thinking on the flight back to New Orleans. The big win they'd just accomplished wasn't enough to change the course of his thoughts. He realized that he had done his best, but it just wasn't working anymore. The truth was, Bum Phillips was tired. Retirement was the only proper course of action.

He knew that his son Wade, an assistant coach with the Saints, would finish out the season if the brass would allow it. If they wouldn't allow it, well, "so be it."

At that moment of decision, Bum Phillips relaxed, the stress lifting from his shoulders. He knew the New Orleans press and fans would be pleased with his retirement announcement. He also knew one other unmistakable fact: "I told everybody that lady'd never spill a beer on my head again and, by golly, I meant it."

Earl had seen this one coming, and wasn't shocked by the news. He knew Bum Phillips, and understood that Bum knew what was best for Bum.

Wade Phillips was given the nod to finish the season as head coach, finishing with a 1-3 record. The team finished the season 5-11, and it was apparent that many changes would take place during the off season in New Orleans. Earl didn't know if he would be part of those changes, but he returned to New Orleans thinking he would give it one more year. He fully intended to remain prepared for any alternative. Earl knew it wouldn't be easy in New Orleans without Bum, and that the new coaches, the press, and all of the fans would be demanding proof that he could still play the game. If any flaw could be found, Earl knew that New Orleans would be unmerciful in their assessment of it, and of him.

The Saints named Jim Mora as their head coach for the 1986 season. Mora was a tough, no-nonsense, well-disciplined coach who understood the challenge that lay ahead of him. The first-year goals he outlined to the media and fans were simple: he intended to get rid of the over-the-hill players on the squad, and to get the Saints into the playoffs. He knew this would be no easy task, but he knew too, that "Rome wasn't built in a day."

The Tyler Rose: The Earl Campbell Story

Immediately after the '85 season was over, Earl returned to work out with Tom Williams. His training with Williams had always prepared him in the past, but Earl realized that the upcoming season would be different and considerably more difficult. As in his senior year at The University of Texas, Earl knew that he had to be in the best shape of his life when going against all the young running backs vying for his job. With this in mind, Williams and Earl worked rigorously. Earl reported to training camp at an extremely well-defined 225 pounds. To all appearances, he looked like the "old Earl," and he was all set to prove the fans and coaches in New Orleans wrong.

Earl knew he would be scrutinized by all the coaches, but he had no idea that Mora would be focusing so intently on him. Mora was looking for any mistakes or deficiencies in Earl's style of play, using him to set an example with his players and to establish himself as the boss. He wanted to weed out all those players who couldn't play according to his guidelines. Thinking back, Earl is convinced that Mora was trying to run him off, in a roundabout way.

Earl remembers August 18, 1986 as if it were just yesterday, since it turned out to be one of the happiest and yet most painful days of his life. It was Saturday, and the Saints were going up against the New England Patriots in their second preseason game. Going into the game, Earl felt good because he would be playing against several of his old friends.

As he'd expected, the friendship was left on the sidelines, as several Patriots were giving the veteran running back particularly intense blows. On one play, Earl was handed the ball and a huge hole opened up. In the past, when such a hole had been presented, the adrenaline would pump and Earl's eyes would bulge with disbelief at his good fortune. But now, after an eight-yard gain, the hole suddenly collapsed, and Earl was brought down hard by the Patriots' defensive unit. Since it was third down and the Saints didn't make the necessary

188

yardage, Earl walked off the field to a smattering of boos.

He stood on the sideline in shock, hoping Mora wouldn't put him in again. Fortunately, he didn't. Earl knew that in the past, he would have blown right through a hole that size, demolishing any defenders who tried to stop him. His performance haunted him for the remainder of the game, for he'd always believed that once he was no longer beneficial to the team, "it was time to pull the pin."

After showering, Earl was so physically sore and bruised that he had a difficult time making it back to the dormitory where the team stayed during training camp. Although his whole body was in pain, it was his feet that hurt the worst. He lay in bed hoping for some relief so that he could sleep. None came. Instead, the pain graduated to intolerable levels, and finally, when Earl had to go to the lavatory, he was forced to crawl on hands and knees to get there. As he crawled, he prayed that God would get him through the night.

After he finally was able to crawl back to bed, with tears of helplessness forming at the corners of his eyes, Earl reached a decision that had been a long time in the making. He'd always known it would happen eventually; he just hadn't anticipated it would happen like this. But the time had come.

Earl picked up the phone and dialed his mother's house in Tyler, hoping she would be awake so he could personally tell her first. His next oldest brother, Alfred, answered instead, and told Earl that their mother had turned in for the night. Alfred would have to be the first to receive the news.

"Alfred, don't wake Momma, but as soon as she gets up in the mornin', tell her that I've decided to retire. Tell her not to be alarmed or worried, because it was my choice." His voice cracked with the emotion of actually speaking the words.

Alfred listened carefully as Earl told him about his decision, and responded as only an understanding older brother could. "Earl, I'm happy for you. All your life, you set certain goals for yourself, and you have achieved each one. You don't need to prove yourself any longer. You've already done that to the entire country. Don't worry about Momma. She'll understand. She's always known that this day would come sooner or later, and she will be pleased to find out it was your choice, not theirs. In the meantime, if there's anything you need, just call and I'll be there. Once again, I'm proud of you, man!"

Earl leaned back after the call, and felt the weight of a world of stress lifted from his shoulders. He was perfectly aware that Alfred was right. Earl Campbell was leaving the game of football on *his* terms, not because of someone else's decision.

Since Earl wanted those closest to him to hear the news first, before he informed the Saints and the media got wind of it, he phoned Darrell Royal next. Coach Royal's wife, Edith, answered the phone and informed Earl that her husband was in Colorado. When Earl explained the reason for his call, she was very understanding, and told Earl that she knew Coach Royal would be pleased to hear about his decision. She promised to get in touch with him immediately, knowing that Darrell would want to talk to Earl as soon as he could. Her last words made Earl positive that he had made the right decision, "You've always been a hero to us, Earl."

Calling Reuna was relatively easy for Earl, for he knew that *she* would be in favor of his decision. Reuna had known for longer than Earl that he had nothing more to prove to anyone. Since the first day she'd met Earl, she had known that he would be a success, and he had proven that to the world over and over again. As he had expected, Reuna was very happy to hear about Earl's decision — happy that the physical abuse to her husband's body would end, and that the Campbells could once again be reunited as a family on a full time basis. She hadn't liked having to live apart after his move to New Orleans to play with the Saints. And as far as she was concerned, Earl's decision couldn't have come at a better time, for she was seven months pregnant with their second child.

New Orleans: The Last Hurrah

The final call of the evening was to Bum Phillips, and Earl knew that this one would be difficult. As Earl suspected, Bum at first thought his good friend was just "joshing" him, because he had played a "darn good game that evening."

When Earl finally convinced Bum that this was a decision he was certain about, Bum's laughter ended. He realized that one of the all-time greatest running backs in professional football was about to hang it up. But Bum, like Ann Campbell, was a realist. He'd known this moment would eventually come, even though he had always believed that Earl would play through the 1986 season.

"Heck, Earl, if that's your decision, I support it one hundred percent. You've done your time, an' done it well. You've done many people proud, includin' myself, an' above everything else, you did it with class. Don't you worry about what the coaches or media say to or about you, just get your stuff an' get on home to your family and friends."

After these four important calls had been made, Earl felt at peace with himself and his decision. He knew he had complete support from those who mattered most to him. He lay back down on his bed once again, and for the first time in a very long time, slept peacefully, knowing that the hardest part of the decision was behind him.

The following day Earl asked Jim Skipper, his running back coach, if he could have a word with him. Skipper agreed, and, as they entered his office for privacy, talked excitedly about how well his backs had performed the previous evening.

"Coach," Earl began, "there's only one way I know how to say somethin', and that's straight up. I'm here to inform y'all that I've decided to retire, effective last night. Bottom line, coach, is that I just don't like playin' football anymore."

Coach Skipper appeared to be honestly shocked by this simple declaration. He tried to talk Earl into rethinking his decision.

"Earl, before you do this, let me go get Coach Mora, so he's aware of what's goin' on."

Earl responded, "I don't care who you go get. I've made up my mind and I'm stickin' by my decision."

Mora came into the room, and upon hearing Earl's decision to retire, appeared as surprised as Skipper had been. Like Coach Skipper, he requested that Earl wait and allow him to talk with Jim Finks, General Manager of the Saints.

Earl told Mora the same thing that he had told Skipper, "Y'all can call whoever you want, I've made my decision and that's it!"

After Finks had spoken to Coach Mora, he called the owner of the team, Tom Benson, at his office in San Antonio. Benson was similarly stunned by Earl's decision, and made plans for an immediate flight to New Orleans. He liked Earl and didn't want to see this happen; in fact, he was one of the few people in the New Orleans organization who felt that Earl could still play. So when Benson met with Earl, he, too, tried, unsuccessfully, to change Earl's mind, even offering him more money on his contract.

"No thanks, Mr. Benson. You've always been fair with me, and I'm gonna be fair with y'all. My mind is made up. I've done my time, and it's important that I go out on my own and that it wasn't someone else's decision." In the back of his mind, Earl had always felt that Coach Mora was going to try to get rid of him eventually, one way or the other.

"Well, heck, Earl. You know I hate to lose you, but if that's your decision, so be it. At least allow us time to contact ESPN and hold an impromptu press conference."

"Tom, I'll do that for y'all, but please make it quick. I wanna get to the airport and home to my family. They need me now, as much as I need them."

"O.K. Earl, good luck. One more thing before you go," Benson said. "I just wanted to say, 'thanks for the memories.'"

"No sweat, Tom. I'll see y'all on down the road."

That afternoon, ESPN and the local media gathered at the press conference where Earl's retirement from professional football was formally announced. The statement was a short and simple *adios* to New Orleans, and to the game that he had loved with all his heart.

Later that year, Earl had an opportunity to speak again with Jim Skipper. Skipper admitted to Earl that he had made a good decision, and had made it at exactly the right time, as Coach Mora had planned to cut him before the season began. Earl was grateful to Skipper for his honesty, and the revelation confirmed that his decision had come not a minute too soon. Earl had gotten to throw the first punch, and a knockout one at that.

Once again, Earl sensed the hand of God in his life. Skipper's coming clean about the situation only served to verify that God had planned for Earl Campbell to retire on his own terms and with dignity.

Earl held no ill feelings toward the city of New Orleans or its fans. He understood that he was being paid big money to perform for these people, and he also knew when the time was right to pull out. Earl figured that the already resentful New Orleans fans would feel cheated had he chosen to play one more year. Ann Campbell's son wouldn't ride somebody's coattails like that, just for the sake of money. If the people in New Orleans had ever bothered to truly get to know The Tyler Rose, they would have realized that he never played football for money.

Earl Campbell played football for *pride*.

After the press conference, Earl boarded the first flight he could get for Houston. Once he was seated, the hostess asked if there was anything she could get for him.

Earl thought for a moment before responding, "Yeah, I'd like six cans of Budweiser."

Shocked, the pretty young attendant informed Earl, "But Mr. Campbell, we're only going to Houston, a forty-minute flight, if that."

Earl smiled, leaning back in his seat as he answered, "I know that, darlin', I know."

When they were airborne, Earl was brought the beer. There are times, after all, when a man just has to celebrate. With the smile seemingly etched on his face, Earl prepared to enjoy the flight home. He never once looked out upon the city or the life he was leaving; instead, he fixed his gaze on the future, and on all the blessings to come. Earl was looking forward to a full-time relationship with his wife, his child, and his child-to-be, and to spending time with his momma and the rest of his family in Tyler. Because of training demands, season schedules, and constant practices that came with a career in professional football, these were pleasures that he hadn't fully experienced in eight years.

With so many positive thoughts in his mind, there was no way Earl could have imagined that God still had a challenge for him, one that had nothing to do with football. Instead, this challenge would literally leave Earl fighting for his life, with no one to help him. This would become, for the famed Tyler Rose, a true test of his will to live.

SECTION VI

LIFE AFTER FOOTBALL

The Tyler Rose: The Earl Campbell Story

"Take it from someone who has experienced this first hand. If you let panic disorder defeat you, the disease loves that. However, when you defeat the disorder, it absolutely despises that!"

Earl Christian Campbell

For the first six months after Earl retired from the glitz and glamour of the NFL, he took a much deserved rest while allowing his beaten and bruised body to heal. He moved back to Houston permanently, and was reunited with Reuna and his son, Christian, to finally become a full time husband and father. This would be the first time his son would have the privilege of having his daddy home all of the time. And on October 26, 1986, Reuna and Earl welcomed their second son, Tyler, into the world.

Because of his celebrity status, Earl was very much in demand for personal appearances and charity causes. He spent countless hours unwinding on numerous golf courses as the guest of many high-powered politicians and wealthy businessmen. Many of the people he met socially would open the door for future business alliances.

Before Earl entered into any business negotiations, he always met with his business advisors, Gardner Parker and Bob Greer, both UT graduates with a definite feel for sound financial endeavors. Earl usually met with these men once a month to plan his strategy for financial independence and to discuss any offers made to him.

It was at one of these monthly meetings that Parker and Greer hit Earl with a "can't-miss" type of proposition relating to The University of Texas and Earl's connection with his alma mater.

Parker and Greer were aware that a person with Earl Campbell's credentials comes around once in a lifetime. In conjunction with Dr. William Cunningham, reigning president of The University of Texas, they confronted Earl with the possibility of going to work in an ambassador type position at UT. Having won the Heisman Trophy, and then excelling in pro ball for eight years, Earl would be ideal for promoting the school to potential recruits, and providing guidance for the young athletes once they arrived on campus.

The proposal seemed like a fantastic opportunity for all in-volved. Earl would be able to show his gratitude to UT for all the school had done for him. He would be able to help the school maintain a superior football program with the "blue chip" athletes who would be drawn by his positive image and his smooth salesman-ship. It was a sure bet that once Earl had a chance to visit with the potential athletes, his presence alone would ensure the signing of choice future Longhorns.

After analyzing the proposal and discussing it with Reuna, Earl realized that there was one drawback, and a major one at that. If he did decide to accept this newly created position at The University of Texas, he would be forced to leave home during the week. He certainly wasn't about to pick up stakes and move his family to Austin without "testing the water" first.

Reuna and Earl decided to give the position a try and if, after six months, it was something that Earl liked to do, *then* they would make the necessary arrangements for a permanent move to Austin. Until that time, they decided that Earl would live in an apartment in Austin, and come home to Houston on Friday evenings. He could spend the weekends with his family, then leave for Austin early Monday morning.

"After only six months' time, I was already leavin' my family again, just like in football," Earl remembers. "Only this time, it was a year-round commitment. There was no way I was gonna do this without a trial period, in case it wasn't for me. So I traveled back and forth from Houston to Austin. The only difference between this job and playin' football was that I would be home on weekends now, instead of preparin' for a game."

Earl's first major assignment in his new position was a young athlete by the name of Eric Metcalf. A skilled running back on the gridiron, Eric was having a difficult time keeping his priorities straight, and the governing powers at UT were considering dismissing the young man from their program. Earl asked for an opportunity to work with Eric, for he saw a lot of himself in the brash, cocky athlete.

Over a period of time, Eric began to heed the advice and emulate the actions of his mentor. Earl often took Eric to Houston with him on weekends. He constantly gave the young man guidance and encouragement, trying to show him the proper protocol to follow if he wished to graduate from college and into a professional football career. Earl knew Eric had that unmistakable talent it takes to play in the NFL, and didn't want him to miss this opportunity.

With Earl's "hands-on" approach, Eric Metcalf developed the discipline and desire to go on to the bright lights and big-dollar contracts of the NFL. Even so, it wasn't until recently, many years after the fact, that Eric finally told Earl and Reuna "thank you" for making him what he is today. He apologized to the Campbells for having waited so long to show his gratitude for their guidance and friendship.

As is typical of him, Earl brushed aside his friend's apology. "No sweat. I understand why it took Eric this long, 'cause I've been there and done that, and I know that one of the hardest things for a professional athlete to do is allow his or her feelin's to be exposed. Heck, I knew Eric would eventually get in touch with us. It was more a question of *when* he would finally find it inside himself to make the call."

Earl will never forget the fateful Friday night that changed his life forever, because the nightmare images keep reappearing, even today. He was en route to Houston after leaving his job in Austin in the early afternoon. He knew from experience that the drive from Austin to Houston took close to three hours, depending upon traffic once he hit the Houston city limits. Yet he always looked forward to the trips home with enthusiasm, anxious to return to his family.

Life After Football

This was the weekend that he planned on telling Reuna and Christian what the new "Campbell game plan" would be, provided, of course, that they all decided it would be best for the family. Earl was truly enjoying his role as ambassador for The University of Texas, and had just about decided he wanted to make it permanent. If he did, of course, a move to Austin was inevitable.

Earl slowed his Mercedes to a stop for the red light at the main intersection in La Grange, a small town halfway between Austin and Houston. He sat with his foot stepping lightly on the brake when suddenly, out of nowhere, a thunderbolt of pain burst in his chest. His heart raced at an alarming level and the pain increased. Earl firmly believed he was having a heart attack.

"I really didn't know what was wrong with me, 'cause it'd never happened before. All I remember is that I was grippin' that steering wheel like it was gonna break off in my hands — *that's* how bad the combination of the pounding and pain was that was goin' on inside my chest. Then I realized how much I was sweatin' and I *knew* I was having a heart attack. I was in too much misery at the time to worry about if anyone could see what was happening to me; but if they did, they knew something was definitely wrong.

"I can't tell y'all how long I sat at the red light, but it seemed like hours. I *do* remember that when it finally went away, I was literally soaked from head to toe, and my foot was stepping so hard on the brake, I could swear it was touching the floorboard. I'll tell y'all what, I just didn't know what to do, or even if I should tell Reuna about it since it coulda been just a fluke. After all, I had just finished playing eight years in the NFL, taking licks from some of the baddest men in the world. It just didn't seem possible that something could be wrong with my health. So, I rationalized that it was a once in a lifetime deal, that it could never happen again. How wrong I turned out to be, don't y'all know!"

Though Reuna was a registered nurse and had extensive training in medicine, Earl had decided against telling her about what had happened to him in La Grange. It was as if by denying it, he would somehow beat the odds of it ever happening again. But the memory of the incident weighed heavily on him, and even after he had showered, Earl didn't have any appetite for supper. He decided just to go to bed and sleep away the entire episode. Sleep eluded him, however; he couldn't get the incident out of his mind. He kept wondering what exactly had happened to him, and he worried about whether it would happen again.

Somewhere in the early morning hours, he finally drifted into a deep sleep. Then, without rhyme or reason, he shot up in bed as if possessed by demons, caught in another excruciatingly painful attack. It came with no warning, but was different than the one he had experienced earlier in the day, because this time both his breathing and his heart rate were affected. Gasping for air, Earl couldn't even speak enough to describe to Reuna what was happening. She had awakened to the sight of her husband, gasping for breath and lying in a pool of sweat. The ferocity of the attack had taken over his entire system.

Reuna watched in horror at what she first believed to be a massive coronary. Fortunately, her schooling paid off, and she didn't panic. Instead, she ran next door to get May Thomas, another registered nurse and a good friend of the Campbell family.

By the time Reuna returned with May, the attack had subsided, but the devastation was reflected in Earl's appearance. His face was drawn with horror at the recurrence of the sudden and mysterious attack, which had disappeared just as quickly as it had begun. He looked much the way he had after the Miami game in his rookie season — totally depleted of energy and severely dehydrated.

After a quick examination, May Thomas and Reuna agreed that Earl had not had a heart attack, but that something was definitely wrong with his body chemistry. May called for Dr. Posey, another neighbor who lived two houses down, to come and examine Earl.

After confirming that May and Reuna were correct in their assessment, Dr. Posey called an ambulance to transfer Earl to St. Luke's Hospital, in the famed Texas Medical Center. Though the attack had subsided, he still carried the terror within him as he was taken from his home on a stretcher.

"Odd," he says contemplatively, "eight years of playin' in the NFL never landed me on a stretcher, yet here I was at the mercy of something totally unknown goin' on inside my body."

As the ambulance crew, with Earl on the stretcher, brushed passed Christian in the hallway, tears streamed down the young boy's cheeks at the sight of his helpless father.

Reuna, too, was having a difficult time accepting the fact that her hero had been stricken with some unspeakably powerful and mysterious force that was capable of throwing him to the ground, when countless men had tried and failed.

Earl remembers his thoughts and feelings as he was being taken out of the house on the stretcher. "I couldn't even say anything to my own son, 'cause I didn't want to lie to him and tell him everything was gonna be all right. Not if *I* wasn't certain whether or not I'd recover from whatever had gotten hold of me."

Over the next week, a seemingly endless series of tests was performed on Earl, as doctors searched for any sign whatever of the heart disease everyone feared. A catheter was even run into his heart to get a clear picture. The results of each test inevitably came back negative; not one revealed even the slightest abnormality. Earl, his physicians, and his family were all mystified.

Earl was beginning to feel like a guinea pig from the poking and prodding, and from all those machines. But the physicians kept coming back to him with the same message, over and over: there was nothing definitive in the test results to indicate a physical problem.

The Tyler Rose: The Earl Campbell Story

When he was finally released from St. Luke's, Earl had no more idea of what was wrong with him, or what had caused his attacks, than he'd had the first night he was admitted. One thing was certain, though: he was scared. This fear was a sensation he hadn't experienced since his father had suddenly died, so many years before.

"The big difference was that when my daddy died," Earl recalls, "I *knew* what I was scared of. With this illness, I didn't have the faintest idea of what I was fightin'. That made the situation all the more confusing."

This was a time of great stress for Reuna too. In addition to trying to figure out some way to get the family moved to Austin, now she was suddenly having to deal with her husband's uncertain health.

And it really seemed that her Earl was a thoroughly beaten man. Eight years in professional football had not been able to cripple him, but this nameless and overwhelming fear had conquered him in a short period of time. Suddenly, he was afraid to go out in public, lest another attack overtake him. He saw no alternative but to take a leave of absence from his position at The University of Texas.

Earl didn't understand what was happening to him as he cringed before his faceless enemy. The medical community had given him no answers and little hope. Earl knew that what was happening to him was real, but he couldn't identify it or fight it. Instead, he withdrew to the shadows of his fear. For an entire month, he sat in his bedroom, behind locked doors and closed curtains, wearing dark glasses to hide the terror in his eyes from those he loved. Many times, he broke down in tears, not from an attack but from the fear of having another one.

Finally, in a moment of total desperation, Earl put in a call to Spanky Stevenson, who had become the head trainer at The University of Texas after Frank Medina retired.

Earl wasted no time on preliminary pleasantries, but whispered his desperate plea into the phone. "Spanky, this is Earl. You gotta minute? 'Cause I really need some help, man!"

"Sure, Earl," Spanky answered cautiously. "Always for you. What's goin' on?"

"Say, man. I don't know if you've heard about anything goin' on with me, but I've been a mess, Spanky. And they can't tell what's wrong with me. Go figure, man. The best doctors in the world, and none of them can figure out what's happenin' inside me. But there's definitely something bad wrong, man. That much I know."

"Tell me what's happening, Earl. Try and describe it to the best of your ability." Spanky was already quite aware that something had to be wrong if Earl was calling for help. It just wasn't Earl's way to ask for anything.

"Well, somethin' comes over me. It makes my heart pound like it's coming outta my chest, and I can't get a full breath. I also break out into a sweat the likes of which you've never seen before, Spanky. It's kinda like a burst of energy that needs to be exorcised from my body, but I have no control over it. I can't even go out to get the paper in the morning, for fear that I'll have one of these attacks. Lord only knows that I don't want Christian to ever see me like that, so I just stay holed up in my bedroom, where it's totally dark and nobody can see me. Please tell me that you know someone that can help me, Spanky. *Please.*"

"Earl. Let's start by you going to see Dr. Lockett. He's a friend of mine and an M.D. I want him to do a full-blown physical on you, listen to the symptoms of your illness, then make a determination on where we should go from there."

"Spanky, man. I've been to the best doctors in the world. They say that, according to all the test results, everything's fine. Do I really gotta go through this again?"

"I hate to say it Earl, but yes, let's start at the very beginning. I'll be in touch with you on a regular basis for an update. In the meantime, I'll also ask around and try to find out everything I can for you. Good luck, my friend."

"O.K. Spanky, thanks. I'll make an appointment to see your friend. Say a prayer for me." Earl would need prayers as he sought answers to one of the most misdiagnosed illnesses in medical history.

His physical examination with Dr. Lockett reconfirmed everything that the prior tests already had ascertained. There was nothing physically wrong inside the body of The Tyler Rose. When Earl described the symptoms of the attack, Dr. Lockett immediately decided that a diagnosis of anxiety disorder could be applied to Earl. The doctor recommended that Earl make an appointment to see Dr. Hauser, a specialist qualified to treat the panic attacks he had been suffering.

Dr. Lockett purposely did not tell Earl that he was being referred to a psychiatrist, knowing the preconceived ideas that some people hold about psychiatry. He knew that Earl must seek immediate help from a qualified specialist, and he didn't want him to be frightened away by the outmoded stigma which still hangs over the mental health field.

Dr. Lockett understood that Earl's illness was one that has to do not only with physical health, but mental health as well, and that the symptoms of panic disorder, while originating from a mental source, are physically very real and profoundly debilitating. The effects of the disease, and the ignorance surrounding it, leave many people who are afflicted by it cringing in fear behind safe walls.

Dr. Lockett was correct in assuming that Earl would misinterpret having been referred to a psychiatrist. When Earl was growing up, psychiatrists were viewed as doctors who treated people who "weren't right in the head." What Earl failed to realize at this stage of his illness was that he *was* suffering from a mental disorder. But like many people, he really didn't have a proper understanding of what the term "mental illness" actually meant.

Education has changed his perspective, however. With educaion, society as a whole is also becoming more knowledgeable and tolerant of people with mental disorders.

"Sometimes," Earl reflects wisely, "this illness has nothing to do with physical handicaps, but it makes me totally incapacitated when it happens."

When Earl and Reuna walked into Dr. Hauser's office, Earl had an uneasy suspicion that everyone was staring at him. His eyes were covered by sunglasses, and he wore a smile to mask his nervousness. Earl remembers that day and grins now as he says, "They were probably starin' at me, 'cause here I was, The Tyler Rose, sittin' in the waiting area of a *psychiatrist's* office."

Before long they were shown into the doctor's consultation room.

"Good afternoon, Mr. and Mrs. Campbell. I'm Dr. Hauser. Dr. Lockett believes I may be able to help you, Mr. Campbell."

"Please, Doctor. Call me Earl. My daddy was 'Mister' Campbell. This is my wife, Reuna. I sure hope you can help me. I've been to hell and back."

As Earl spoke, he did a quick once-over of Dr. Hauser, observing the GQ-looking suit, the expensive shoes, the jewelry — "the whole nine yards," as he describes it. Earl had long been wary of high rollers, and immediately judged that Dr. Hauser fit into this category. Remembering that first meeting, Earl says that he probably gave the man a real fit.

For his part, Hauser had seen many patients with Earl's symptoms. Observing Earl with his sunglasses on, and noting his restless behavior, the obvious physical drain from lack of sleep, and the extreme weight loss, Dr. Hauser knew what was wrong with him. He also knew this new patient needed help in a hurry, but first he must win Earl's trust and confidence. He sensed, though, that even after this was accomplished, Earl would be reluctant to accept being told that he, a larger-than-life star, had mental problems. Earl had never understood, nor taken kindly to, any allusion to mental weakness on his part.

Dr. Hauser explained to Earl that he was experiencing the classic symptoms associated with panic disorder, or P.D. for short. He said that this problem could have developed for a number of reasons, and that the disease can lie dormant for years and then be triggered by one simple, seemingly insignificant occurrence. The doctor further explained that the illness originates as the result of mental or brain abnormalities, typically an imbalance in the brain's own chemistry. Hauser reassured Earl that the field of knowledge in this area was expanding daily, and that new treatments and medications had been developed to address the needs of patients suffering from panic disorder.

Dr. Hauser could see Earl stiffen each time a reference was made to a mental disorder, but he continued with his explanation, telling Earl that simple stress often escalates into a form of panic disorder. In Earl's case, there could have been a number of causes. He noted that Earl had recently retired from a high-profile position in professional football. This alone was stressful, and then there was the normal anxiety about moving to a different city, coupled with the recent birth and added responsibility of a second child.

Dr. Hauser continued, noting that Earl's face had gone pale and his breathing had become irregular. There was bad news and good news about panic attacks, he said. The bad news was that the onset of the attacks could not be predicted, but the good news was that they *could* be treated, with proper medication and various breathing and relaxation techniques.

Dr. Hauser then told Earl that he wanted to prescribe a new medication called Prozac® to help Earl with his disorder. He explained to Earl that it would take a little time for the Prozac to change his brain chemistry enough to realize beneficial results, and once it did, there was a good possibility that the dosage would have to be gradually increased and then closely monitored.

It was no easy task telling Earl Campbell, the football great, that he would now have to be under the continuing care of a psychiatrist. But, for Earl, it was no easy task to hear it either. In fact, Earl couldn't believe what he was hearing.

"First this GQ wannabe was tellin' us that my attacks were mental; that I'm a nut case. Then, after he tells us this, he immediately wants to start me on some drug. Y'all know that I don't like drugs, 'cause I'm scared I'll get addicted to them. You had to know that it was hard to accept when Hauser told me that I was sick in the head, 'cause crazy is one thing that I've never been accused of bein'."

Earl remembers telling Dr. Hauser, "I gotta be honest with you, 'cause that's the only way I know how to be. I didn't realize that you were a psychiatrist or I probably wouldn't have come here today. I'm havin' a real hard time sittin' here with you tellin' me that this monster that's overtaken my body is all in my mind."

Dr. Hauser was patient with Earl, and explained to him that he was misunderstanding the diagnosis. He explained that the attacks are not all in the mind, that these attacks are very real to the people experiencing them, and that the physical ramifications of the disorder can be devastating. Earl nodded when he heard Dr. Hauser explain this, because the fear of having those physical symptoms return was haunting him.

Anxiety disorder can lead to other disorders as well, both physical and mental, and depression can develop just from the fear of having another attack. Patients slowly withdraw from the normal life they once had because of the fear and anxiety. Dr. Hauser equated anxiety disorder to a fingerprint, because no two patients' symptoms or reactions are identical. He said that anxiety disorder is a very individualized illness. He continued to reassure Earl that with certain medications such as Prozac, the illness could be controlled and the fear diminished.

Dr. Hauser could see Earl's jaw clench. The silence was long, as Hauser waited for his explanation to sink in. He knew from experience that patients needed time to think and deal with such an unexpected and unsettling prognosis. He understood that Earl's emotions were splintered.

Finally, Earl replied, "All right, Doctor. I'm gonna give this drug a chance based on how positive you are that it can help me get back to normal. However, I hope the good Lord above sees to it that I don't get hooked and have *that* monkey on my back too. I'll give your drug one month, but I'll be by twice a week to see you. If y'all don't mind, do ya think I could come straight up to your office? I'm havin' a hard time dealin' with all of this and I don't want people to think I'm nuts 'cause I'm here."

Earl left Dr. Hauser's office and immediately started on the Prozac. Still very fearful of the side effects of this medication, and somewhat leery of Dr. Hauser's assessment, he made an appointment with another psychiatrist — without Dr. Hauser's knowledge — to confirm the original diagnosis.

Over the course of the next several months, Earl stopped seeing the other psychiatrist. He explains, "He tried to use me as a guinea pig. He decided that my problem was from all the caffeine in the coffee that I was drinkin' and wanted me to do all kinda crazy experiments. After only a couple of his experiments, I said *adios* to that doctor."

With the daily medication and his twice weekly office visits, Earl realized that his panic attacks were decreasing in number and severity with each passing day. For Earl, life was finally beginning to have some semblance of normalcy again.

Since Earl had always been a very physical being, the relaxation techniques and breathing exercises particularly appealed to him. After several months, he decided it was time to test his physical well-being, his behavior modification techniques, and the effectiveness of his medication. So one morning Earl stepped outside his house, venturing as far as his neighbor's mailbox. Each day, he would add one additional neighbor's mailbox to his walk, until he was finally able to walk the entire block. Then he could walk two blocks, and then three.

Finally, after many frightening months, Earl was able to "run" in the neighborhood, and run he did! He finally felt free of the demons that had taken over his body. With the help of his medication and exercise, he had soundly defeated them.

Dr. Hauser eventually took Earl off the daily dose of Prozac and placed him on Zanax® three times daily. Fortunately, Reuna was usually around to remind Earl to take his medication, because, as he got stronger, he would forget to take it regularly. When this happened, the attacks would reoccur. But Reuna would always be at Earl's side to help him with the breathing techniques and to reassure him.

With the professional help of Dr. Hauser, the love and support of Reuna and his family, the necessary medication, and the breathing techniques and relaxation exercises, Earl again gained control. He firmly believes, "This is an illness that can't be beaten. It can only be controlled. How do I know this? 'Cause I still have the attacks if I don't stay on top of it, at all times."

Earl's experience with panic disorder has undoubtedly left him a changed man. He holds tremendous respect for public figures like John Madden and Willard Scott who, much like himself, have acknowledged that they suffer from this illness, and are willing to discuss it openly. Each of them has overcome the stigma that is so often attached to mental illness, and now they encourage others to come forward and seek help.

Earl eventually went back to his job at The University of Texas. After seeking medical help and taking medication, he was no longer embarrassed because of the disease and, over time, has become increasingly comfortable when discussing panic disorder. He has helped many other sufferers come to terms with their condition, and has helped educate a public that is still somewhat intolerant of mental illness.

In fact, Earl averages 150 speaking engagements per year, many of these delivered to audiences who suffer from panic disorder. He has learned to confront and control the disorder in the same way he played football: aggressively. He visualizes his audience as his teammates, and panic disorder as the opposing team. Together, Earl tells his audience, they can defeat the opposition.

Earl delivers a personal testimony about his battle with panic disorder and how he learned to control its symptoms. He tells those in his audience who are afflicted with the disorder that they must constantly strive to defeat the disease, one day at a time. He encourages them to seek professional help, get on the proper medication, learn behavior modification, develop an exercise program, and learn to do the breathing and relaxation techniques. But he is also quick to add that without his belief in a Higher Power, his recovery would have failed.

"Sixty-five percent of panic disorder is within the person," Earl declares to his interested listeners. "Because it is a mentally induced illness, the individuals who suffer from it *must* defeat it themselves. No one else can do it for them. That's the downside, 'cause if you're not strong enough inside, then the illness will surely succeed.

"The real problem arises from those who understand they suffer from the disorder but don't seek help. Since it is a relatively recent diagnosis by the medical experts, we don't have a true understanding of how many people are out there who won't come forward. It's not 'cause they don't want to. They're just scared, like I once was. The reason I speak on panic disorder so often is that I might induce others to seek help. If this happens, I consider it another defeat suffered by the illness 'cause I realize that I am involved in another game now, one that never ends for me or others who suffer from panic disorder.

"Until such time as they (doctors) can figure out a permanent cure for this illness, the object of this game will be to stay even or ahead at all times, never allowing for the demons located inside our minds to gain control of the situation. This game has no trophies or awards. Life itself is the determining factor for those who choose to participate."

In 1990, Tommy Harmon asked Earl if he would have dinner with a couple of his friends so they could discuss a possible business proposal. Harmon was a friend of Earl's who had played baseball at UT before going on to play for the Philadelphia Phillies. He had retired to live in Fort Worth. Earl agreed and met Pat Poehl and Jerry Klossner at Schultz's Beergarten, a popular Austin hangout for UT students and alumni.

The two men approached Earl with a unique idea for an industrial waste removal business, and asked him if he would be interested in becoming a partner with them. But because of the volatile political overtones often associated with industrial waste, especially in the state capital (and environmentally aware city) of Austin, Earl was immediate and adamant in his response.

"I told them I didn't want any part of industrial waste. It was way too hot of an issue for me."

Pat Poehl tossed another idea to Earl. "Word has it that you know a lot about sausage, and that you know how to make some of the best in the state of Texas. Is that a fact?"

"Heck yeah, man. I know how to mix up some of the best, spiciest sausage ever eaten. That *is* a fact. I also know how to prepare some of the best barbecue ribs you ever sank your teeth into, if you really wanna know!"

"I'll tell you what, Earl. Why don't we all get together and mix some up to see what *other* folks think about it? Maybe we could

The Tyler Rose: The Earl Campbell Story

stimulate some interest in a food that has been created and prepared by The Tyler Rose. If your sausage and ribs are as good as you say they are, who knows what could come of this?"

And so it was that Earl, Pat, and Jerry soon started serving up Earl Campbell's special recipe of sausage and ribs after UT football games, holding tailgate parties in the parking lot of Memorial Stadium. They'd park their truck outside the main gate, where people would have to walk by (and catch the aroma of) the smoke pit that was used to cook the fine-tasting meats. The reaction from virtually everybody who tried the uniquely seasoned sausage and ribs was overwhelmingly enthusiastic. So Earl, Pat, and Jerry decided to expand their enterprise and take their idea to the next level: they began serving the sausage and ribs to customers at Schultz's Beergarten.

It was like the tailgate giveaway all over again. "People went absolutely crazy over the stuff," Earl recalls. "Pretty soon they began calling local radio stations, wantin' to know where they could get some of that Earl Campbell 'sausage on a stick.' Our big break came at Schultz's, though, 'cause one of the people who tried it had a father-in-law who was the senior buyer for Appletree food stores. He bragged so much to his father-in-law about how good the sausage was that I got a call from the man inquirin' about my recipe. Well, one thing led to another and I agreed to fly to Houston and meet with him. Of course, I brought along a Styrofoam cooler filled with the sausage and ribs.

"At this point, I really didn't know what to expect, especially since the man told me his wife was actually the connoisseur of homemade sausage and that he would like *her* to try it before making any decisions. Ya gotta understand that, at that point, I didn't understand what decisions this man was talkin' about makin'. That is, until his wife tried my recipe that night. I remember that Reuna had forgotten to tell me he had called while I was on my return flight to Austin, and I was kinda bummed out. The next day, when she remembered to tell me, my heart began poundin', but this time it wasn't from anxiety. It was from a rush of adrenaline. I immediately called the man and he told me his wife said it was 'the best sausage she had ever eaten.'

"That was back in 1990. From that point forward, the rest is history since Jerry, Pat and myself made a deal with J.B. Sausage in Wealder, Texas to manufacture and package my sausage. We started small, mainly stocking it in the Appletree stores; but, in what seems like no time all, we went from 600 pounds a month to well over 600,000 pounds in some months today. I guess you could say that Earl Campbell Foods is now a success story in and of itself. But I give a lot of credit to Jerry and Pat. They stuck in there and plugged away with me. We each had sort of a dream about this, and now it seems like that dream has come full circle."

With characteristic modesty, Earl was downplaying how popular his sausage has become. Earl Campbell Foods is still something of a Texas secret, since many people outside the state can't get it. However, many popular athletes such as Dennis Rodman call and have the sausage shipped to them. The limited availability problem is likely to change in the near future, as Earl Campbell Foods is negotiating a deal with a large food chain to distribute the products nationwide.

Of all the accomplishments Earl reflects back upon, Earl Campbell Foods is perhaps the greatest, for it allowed him to prove to himself as well as many others that he could be as successful off the football field as on it.

"I always said that someday I'd make a million dollars outside of football. With the good Lord's blessin', I now have that opportunity and am doing my best to see it through."

Each year, during Super Bowl weekend, Earl Campbell appears as a guest celebrity and spokesperson at the Flamingo Hilton in Las Vegas. He is one of the most popular celebrities at the Flamingo, because he always finds times for pictures and autographs with his fans. He likes to take the time to recognize those fans who still stop to cheer him on.

It was on January 29, 1991, Super Bowl Sunday, while at the Hilton, that Earl's life again changed dramatically. The Denver Broncos were preparing to do battle against the San Francisco 49er's, and Earl was just about to head downstairs for the festivities. As he was leaving, the phone began ringing. Earl considered ignoring it, but fortunately chose otherwise. "Yes?" he answered when he picked up the receiver.

"Earl, is that you?"

"Yeah, man. Who's this?"

"This is Ron Coleman, down here in Austin. Have you heard the news yet?" Coleman was an Austin sportswriter.

"No. What news?" Since arriving the day before, Earl had much more on his mind than taking time out of his schedule to watch television or read the newspaper.

"Well," Coleman said, clearly amazed at Earl's reply, "I guess I'm the first one, then. Congratulations, Earl, you've been voted into the Pro Football Hall of Fame! I just got wind of it and decided to try and reach you for an interview. Do you have some time now, or can I get back to you?"

"Uh, I'm supposed to be downstairs right now, so I'm already late. Do me a favor, Ron. Call me back this evening and I'll talk about it then. I hate to do this, but I really gotta run, man."

Earl was floored by the news, but didn't have time to let it really sink in at that moment. He spent the rest of the day being a gracious host, talking to fans and signing autographs. Although people stopped to congratulate him all afternoon about his most recent honor, the full impact of this news didn't sink in until he was back in his suite alone.

"Ya know, when it finally sank in, *that's* when the adrenaline rush hit me," he says. "I was all alone and reminiscin' about what I had accomplished since being outta football, and this further served to solidify the respect I had earned from those who coached and played, not only with me; but, as I've said before, *those who coached and played against me*. I remember thinkin' about something Joe Greene once said: 'When the best don't meet the best, then nobody will know who the best is.' It finally sank in what he was tryin' to say, 'cause many people had voted to make me one of the best."

Two weeks later, Earl and his family flew to Hawaii for the annual Pro Bowl. All five of the newly appointed inductees into the Hall of Fame were present with their families for the formal announcement before a national television audience.

The other honorees besides Earl were Jan Stenerud, Stan Jones, John Hannah, and "Tex" Schramm. Jan Stenerud was the first kicker inducted into this prestigious fraternity of gifted athletes, after playing many years with Kansas City, Green Bay, and Minnesota. Stan Jones had played guard for several years with the Chicago Bears and Washington Redskins, during a time when men actually believed in allegiance to the city they played for instead of "who was willing to pay the highest price.'" John Hannah had played guard for the New England Patriots, and was known for laying down some of the sweetest blocks a running back could ever envision. Finally, there was "Tex" Schramm, who helped create the mystique of "America's Team." Tex was revered as the powerful General Manager of the world renowned Dallas Cowboys.

Standing on that field in Hawaii, Earl once again felt an incredible sense of pride at what he had been able to accomplish — but he still hadn't experienced the full impact of the award, the part that would forever change the outcome of The Tyler Rose's life. That wouldn't happen until the actual day of induction, July 27, 1991.

When the time was approaching, Earl rented a couple of minivans to take the female members of his family on a well-deserved vacation. Their final destination was to be Canton, Ohio, home of the Professional Football Hall of Fame. Many of Earl's other friends would also be present for the ceremony, some making long journeys from all areas to be there when this special award was given to their comrade.

The July afternoon was extremely hot for Ohio. The heat was particularly intense for Earl because, as a visual symbol of their achievement, each inductee was given a heavy beige sport coat to wear for the ceremony.

Earl had asked his ex-coach and good friend, Bum Phillips, to make the introduction to his acceptance speech. And Bum addressed the onlookers and the national TV audience in the same humble, down-home way he always spoke.

"I'd like to take credit for Earl Campbell and for all he's meant to football but, truth about it, the credit belongs to the other people that raised him. His junior high coaches, his momma Ann, his sisters and his whole family. They're the ones that did the job. Believe me, when I got Earl Campbell, he was not only a football player — already — he knew how to live on the field *and* off the field, and it's a credit to his family and to the people who've brought him up."

Bum paused a moment, trying to check the emotion welling up inside him. "Every time you see Earl Campbell sign an autograph, you'll see him sign it, then he'll look up, look you in the eye, ask you your name, and he'll take the time with ya', an' make sure that you understand that he's as proud you asked him as he is to sign it. Believe me, those are the things that I think about Earl Campbell. Y'all can watch him in the movies — an' I can watch him in my memory. I've got a lotta memories, been around a long time. I think about it a lot, an' when I stop an' think about it, Earl Campbell, you are my greatest memory of all!"

Earl joined the crowd in appreciation of Bum's kind words. Then it was his turn, standing to address the audience. For the first

say, 'Earl, I'm through with you, son.' But she reminds me of a song that Willie Nelson and Merle Haggard wrote called, '*Old Tougher Than Leather,*' and that's my wife, Reuna.

"I'm so proud to be an American. I'm so proud to be in the Hall of Fame with the Jim Browns, the Franco Harris's, and someday soon, I'm sure, the Walter Paytons and the Tony Dorsetts. But when they say *Campbell*, I want y'all to remember this: 'The old boy gave his all. *Who Will Buy My Memories?* as Willie Nelson says. Thank you."

And with that, The Tyler Rose raised his right hand skyward, displaying a closed fist. Only his forefinger and little finger stood straight into the air. It was, of course, the famous "Hook 'Em 'Horns" sign, for all his friends from The University of Texas, and all across America, to see.

Ann and B. C.'s boy, Earl Christian Campbell — a black kid from deep in the Texas Piney Woods, a Heisman Trophy winner, and a hero both on and off the field — had stepped into his place in history in the Pro Football Hall of Fame. It was an honor reserved for only the best of the best among American athletes.

After the induction ceremony, Earl reluctantly bid good-bye to his family and friends on their return trip. He couldn't join them, as he was scheduled to be in Minnesota for a fund-raising banquet the next day. But he was too tired to think about that or anything else as he entered another faceless hotel room for the night.

He was sitting on the end of the bed, awaiting the bellhop's return with a bucket of ice that he had requested. When the young man returned with the ice, Earl attempted to hand him a tip, but was stopped in the process when the boy announced, "I couldn't accept that from you, Mr. Hall of Famer."

With that, the bellboy turned and walked out the door, leaving Earl speechless, the many thoughts in his mind silenced by the rush of emotion he felt. It was on this night, at this moment, in a hotel room that was simultaneously everywhere and nowhere at all, that he finally was able to accept his father's passing, so many years before. He realized, at last, that he could think good thoughts about his father and remember the good times. B.C. Campbell was, in that moment of solitude and tears, finally laid to rest. And Ann's boy Earl had only just begun . . . .

THE END

APPENDICES

APPENDIX I
EARL CHRISTIAN CAMPBELL:
CHRONOLOGICAL LIST OF ACCOMPLISHMENTS

1972-1973

■ All-American linebacker at John Tyler High School — Junior year

■ All-American running back at John Tyler High School — Senior year (rushed for 2,224 yards)

■ John Tyler High School wins State Championship, remaining undefeated throughout the season

1974

■ Southwest Conference Newcomer of the Year (950 yards rushing as a freshman)

■ All Southwest Conference at The University of Texas

1975

■ All Southwest Conference at The University of Texas

■ All-American at The University of Texas

1977

■ All Southwest Conference at The University of Texas

■ All-American at The University of Texas

■ Heisman Trophy Winner, accumulating 4,443 total rushing yards in four years at The University of Texas

1978

■ First pick of the NFL draft by the Houston Oilers

■ NFL Rookie of the Year

■ Most Valuable Player of the NFL

■ NFL Rushing Title, rushing for 1,450 yards

■ Voted All Pro in NFL

■ Selected as Pro Bowl Player

1979

- His #20 Longhorn jersey is the only jersey in the history of The University of Texas to be retired (November 24, 1979)
- Most Valuable Player of the NFL
- NFL Rushing Title, rushing for 1,697 yards
- Voted All Pro in NFL
- Selected as Pro Bowl Player

1980

- Most Valuable Player of NFL
- NFL Rushing Title, rushing for 1,934 yards
- Voted All Pro in NFL
- Selected As Pro Bowl Player
- Rushed for 1,934 yards (third highest in the NFL)
- Four 200 yard rushing games
- Eleven 100 yard rushing games

1981

- Voted All Pro in NFL
- Selected as Pro Bowl Player
- Texas State Legislature passes a bill proclaiming Earl Campbell as the fourth official State Hero of Texas

1982

- Voted All Pro in NFL
- Selected as Pro Bowl Player

1983

- Voted All Pro in NFL
- Selected as Pro Bowl Player
- Rushed for over 1,000 yards five of his first six seasons

1984

- Voted All Pro in NFL

1987

- Campbell's #34 jersey retired by the Houston Oilers, August 13

1990

■   Inducted into the College Football Hall of Fame

1991

■   Inducted into the Pro Football Hall of Fame

1996

■   Inducted into the Texas College Football Hall of Fame

NFL Career Totals:

■   9,407 total yards rushing

■   806 total yards receiving

■   74 total touchdowns

■   10,213 combined net total yardage

■   Ranks #10 as all time rusher in the NFL

■   Appeared on the cover of *Sports Illustrated* six times

APPENDIX II
WHERE ARE THEY NOW?

Fred Akers: Executive with Pacific Institute.

Ann Campbell: Happily watching her grandchildren develop. The street her house sits on has been renamed "Ann Campbell Lane," as a tribute to what she has accomplished in her lifetime and for society.

Earl Campbell: On a mission to do as much as he can for mankind.

Raymond Clayborn: Marketing Representative, Players Casino, Lake Charles, La.
NFL, retired, 15 years.

George Craddock: Retired Tyler I.S.D. Coached for twenty years.

Ken Dabbs: Retired from The University of Texas after 22 years. Spent 12 years as recruiter and coach; final 10 in administration. Currently involved with synthetic turf for athletic facilities.

Conway Hayman: Instructor and assistant football coach, Prairie View A&M, Prairie View, Texas.

Rick Ingraham:	Sales Manager, Industrial Equipment, Dallas, Texas.
Jerry Klossner:	Partner, Earl Campbell Foods, Inc.
Lawrence La Croix:	Deceased; memory lives on in the hearts of many.
Thorndike Lewis:	Assistant principal at John Tyler High School. Still does it for the kids.
Carl Mauck:	Retired NFL. Currently an assistant coach with the Phoenix Cardinals.
Frank Medina:	The University of Texas Athletic Department (Deceased).
Louie Murillo:	Still employed with The University of Texas Athletic Department.
Corky Nelson:	Coach, Seguin High School, Seguin, Texas. Thirty-one years of coaching and still going.
Gifford Nielsen:	Sports Director, KHOU-TV, Houston, Texas. Color Analyst for Oiler Radio Network, KTRH.
Ernest & Joyce Owens:	Semi-retired in Dallas, Texas. Enjoying trips on their bus.

Gardner Parker: President, Parker Investments,
Houston, Texas.

"Bum" Phillips: Retired NFL coach. Currently residing in
Goliad, Texas.
Does what he damn well pleases.

Pat Poehl: Partner, Earl Campbell Foods, Inc.

Darrell Royal: Retired, enjoying golf.

ABOUT THE AUTHOR

Paddy Joe Miller resides in Spring, Texas with his wife, Jan, and daughter, Linsey. A 1977 graduate of Bloomsburg University in Pennsylvania, Paddy is a prolific writer. This is his third published work. The first, *Lies in the Family Album*, an autobiographical account of Miller's incredible search for his biological father, was the catalyst that brought him and Earl Campbell together to create this biography. In his second book, a gripping novel called *Cash, Credit, or Murder Accepted*, the author exposes an underworld within the automobile business, which leads to both mystery and murder.

By this writing of *The Tyler Rose*, Paddy Joe Miller hopes that everyone will realize that with honesty, hard work, and love, anything in life is possible.

time in a very long time, Earl experienced butterflies in his stomach as he looked over to where his momma was sitting, proudly admiring her sixth child.

The Tyler Rose composed himself before beginning what was to become an extremely emotional speech.

"Every team I've ever played on, I've always tried to share with the guys that I played with. And I think, if any of them had anything to say about Earl Campbell, they'd say he's a giver. He's not a taker!

"And there goes my mother, Mrs. Ann Campbell. I was listenin' to her, coming back to the hotel. She has seven boys and four girls; I'm number six in the family. I said, 'Ya know, everything's good; it's amazing how God blesses you.' She said, 'Yes, I remember one Sunday morning when I was gettin' you dressed for church. I told your daddy I wasn't ever gonna get a chance to go anywhere, I wasn't ever gonna have a chance to see anything. He says, "Darlin', you oughta be careful, 'cause you never know what God has in store for you!"' Then she says, 'Who'd of thought I'd be here in Canton, Ohio?'

"I didn't even think *I* was gonna be here, Momma. But, I'm happy you're here!" The crowd laughed as Earl gestured toward his mother.

"The more and more I try an' write a speech, the one thing I'll always remember about this day — beyond football — is that my daddy, B.C. Campbell, is up there in heaven, I believe, with all his buddies, an' he's tellin' them what a great son he has. 'Look at my son, I know he can handle it.' And I thank y'all so much — for everything." At this point, Earl briefly lost control over his emotions and had to pause to allow the tears behind his sunglasses to dry before he could continue.

"Every day is not a great day in my life. I mean, I'm like everybody else. I work hard, an' that's all I ever do. I've got a lady that's been with me twenty-four years, if I'm right. You stay with them so long, you kinda forget it, but if it was me, some days I'd just